Das große Testübungsbuch
Englisch

© für diese Ausgabe
by Naumann & Göbel Verlagsgesellschaft mbH
Emil-Hoffmann-Straße 1
D-50996 Köln
Autor: Alexander Peter Saccaro
Redaktion: Oliver Christian Weber
Gesamtherstellung: Naumann & Göbel Verlagsgesellschaft mbH, Köln
Alle Rechte vorbehalten

VORWORT

Hallo liebe Schülerin, hallo lieber Schüler!

In diesem Übungsbuch findest du über 100 Englischtests, die dir bei der Vorbereitung auf Klassenarbeiten und Tests helfen sollen und die gleichzeitig Schritt für Schritt deine Englischkenntnisse verbessern. Das Buch enthält den Unterrichtsstoff von zwei Schuljahren. Der Stoff wird in den Schulen in unterschiedlicher Reihenfolge behandelt, daher empfehlen wir dir, immer einen Test zu dem Thema herauszusuchen, das du auch gerade im Unterricht durchnimmst.

Es bringt nicht viel, kurz vor einer Klassenarbeit den ganzen Stoff schnell auswendig zu lernen. Viel besser ist es, regelmäßig und in kleinen, übersichtlichen Portionen zu lernen. Daher sind die Tests immer nur eine Seite lang und dauern nicht lange.

Wenn du etwa an jedem zweiten Schultag einen Test machst, wird dir das wirklich helfen. Suche dir einen Test zu einem Thema aus, das dich sehr interessiert. Oder du wählst ein Thema, das ihr gerade in der Schule durchnehmt. Nimm dir für das Bearbeiten einer Testseite und das Studieren der Lösungen etwa 25 Minuten Zeit. Bitte benutze zum Ausfüllen der Testseiten einen Bleistift, denn dann kannst du die Lösungen leicht wegradieren und den Test so mehrfach wiederholen.

So arbeitest du mit dem Übungsbuch:
- Im Inhaltsverzeichnis sind **alle wichtigen Themen des 5. und 6. Schuljahrs** übersichtlich aufgelistet. Auf jeder Testseite findest du den Lernbereich im farbigen Balken oben auf der Seite und das Thema in der Testüberschrift.
- Die Tests sind in **3 Schwierigkeitsstufen** eingeteilt. An den farbigen Kästchen erkennst du, ob ein Test leicht ■ □ □, mittelschwierig ■ ■ □ oder schwierig ■ ■ ■ ist.
- Anhand der **ausführlichen Lösungen** kannst du überprüfen, ob du alles richtig gemacht hast. Du findest sie am Ende des Buches.
- **Tipps** (wie bei Test 17) helfen dir bei besonders kniffligen Aufgaben auf die Sprünge.
- Das Übungsbuch ist so aufgebaut, dass du dir einzelne Tests zu bestimmten **Themen** heraussuchen kannst. Du musst das Buch nicht von vorn nach hinten durcharbeiten. Bei Themen, die du schwierig findest, solltest du immer ganz am Anfang des Themas beginnen. Bei leichteren Themen kannst du auch mit ■ ■ □- oder ■ ■ ■-Aufgaben einsteigen.

Wir wünschen dir viel Spaß und Erfolg!

INHALTSVERZEICHNIS

Wortarten

Das Substantiv

Die Begleiter

Das Adjektiv

Präpositionen

Pronomen

Adverbien

Mengen, Zahlen und Daten

Mengenangaben

Zahlen und Daten

INHALTSVERZEICHNIS

INHALTSVERZEICHNIS

Test 1

☐ Schwierigkeitsstufe

Das Substantiv – *Singular und Plural*

Regelmäßige Pluralbildung

1. Bilde den Plural der folgenden Substantive.

book	*books*	plan	*planes*
plane	*planes*	minute	*minutes*
answer	*answers*	apple	*apples*
face	*faces*	chair	*chairs*
box	*boxes*	dress	*dresses*
table	*tables*	page	*pages*
sandwich	*sandwiches*	pencil case	*pencilcases*
bridge	*bridges*	desk	*desks*
hour	*hours*	brush	*brushes*
teacher	*teaches*	pupil	*pupils*

Beachte die Aussprache!

2. Bei welchen der folgenden Substantive wird die Pluralendung wie /iz/ ausgesprochen? Unterstreiche diese Substantive.

pages	exercises	churches	<u>clothes</u>	<u>houses</u>
faces	roles	<u>stages</u>	theatres	buses
<u>titles</u>	languages	phrases	<u>pieces</u>	centres
bridges	cornflakes	messages	places	<u>brochures</u>
voices	noises	<u>noses</u>	horses	scenes
brushes	cakes	classes	glasses	tables

Test 2

| Schwierigkeitsstufe |

Das Substantiv – *Singular und Plural*

Und wie steht es mit dem Singular?

1. **Bilde den Singular der folgenden Substantive.**

days	_____	boys	_____
babies	_____	families	_____
thieves	_____	plays	_____
wives	_____	knives	_____
shelves	_____	countries	_____
parties	_____	lives	_____
halves	_____	hobbies	_____

Und noch einmal zum Plural

2. **Setze die folgenden Substantive in den Plural.**

a boy and a girl _____

a brother and a sister _____

a book on a shelf _____

a pupil and a teacher _____

a cat and a dog _____

a short life _____

a baby and a toy _____

a night and a day _____

a diary and a pen _____

a house and a flat _____

a bus and a lorry * _____

* lorry = Lkw (American English: truck = trucks)

Test 3

▮▮☐ Schwierigkeitsstufe

Das Substantiv – *Singular und Plural*

Besonderheiten

1. **Wie lautet der Plural?**

   child _____   country _____

   sheep _____   cake _____

   sandwich _____   knife _____

   man _____

Achte auf die richtige Schreibweise

2. **Ergänze die fehlenden Buchstaben.**

   You can stand on one f _____ .

   What you eat, is your f _____ .

   For most people the first meal in the morning is b _____ .

   Your father and mother are your p _____ .

   Father, mother and children are a f _____ .

   The people who live next door are your n _____ .

Test 4

Schwierigkeitsstufe

Das Substantiv – *Singular und Plural*

Besonderheiten

1. Einige der folgenden Substantive sehen wie Singulare, andere wie Plurale aus. Wie musst du sie gebrauchen? Trage die folgenden Substantive bitte in die entsprechenden Rubriken ein.

   news   information   people

   mathematics   police   homework

   nur im Singular   **nur im Plural**

   _____ _____

   _____ _____

   _____ _____

   _____ _____

Was ist richtig?

2. Vervollständige die Sätze, indem du die richtige Form von *to be* einträgst.

   a) There _____ too much homework. We really can't do it.

   b) There are some people who think that homework _____ fun.

   c) These people _____ completely wrong, I can tell you.

   d) What's the homework for today? Well, there _____ some maths homework, and there _____ homework in English, German and Biology.

   e) That _____ bad news again. But thanks for the information though* it _____ not very good.

   * though = obwohl

Test 5

Schwierigkeitsstufe

Das Substantiv – s-Genitiv und of-Genitiv

Und wie steht es mit diesen Substantiven?

1. Gebrauche den s-Genitiv.

a man / world _____

women / magazines _____

a woman / job _____

men / hobbies _____

children / playground _____

a child / toys _____

people / ideas _____

girls / day _____

Vermischtes ...

2. Verbinde die Substantive mit dem s-Genitiv.

Are these your **teeth**? No, they are _____ (grandpa)

Is this your **baby**, Alice? No, it's my _____ (sister)

Are these your **parents**? No, they are _____ (Tom)

Are these your **jeans**? No, they are _____ (that girl)

Are these your **children**, Mrs Benson? No, they are _____ (Mr Owen)

Is that your **mum**, Ken? No, it's _____ (that boy)

Is this your hamster's **cage**? No, it's _____ (my parrot)

Is this your sister's **doll**? No, it's the _____ (twins)

Is this your child's **food**? No, it's _____ (the cat)

Test 6   Schwierigkeitsstufe

Das Substantiv – s-Genitiv und of-Genitiv

Der of-Genitiv

1. Verbinde die folgenden Substantive mit dem of-Genitiv. Achte darauf, welches Substantiv zuerst kommen muss.

   the table/the legs _____

   the book/the month _____

   your eyes/the colour _____

   this book/the pages _____

   the apple/my eye _____

   the photos/my sister _____

   the room/the walls _____

   this house/the roof _____

   the girl/my dreams _____

   this word/the plural _____

   this exercise/the end _____

Toms Freund

2. a) Unterstreiche das Genitiv-s mit einer anderen Farbe als das Apostroph-s der Kurzformen.

   Tom's got a new friend. He's the new boy in Tom's class. Ken's family is new here, too. Ken's very good at maths. He can be very helpful, so most pupils in Tom's class like him. Ken's got a pet, too. It's a hamster. He must look after it, clean its cage and buy the hamster's food.

   b) Schreibe die Kurzformen aus.

   _____

   _____

Test 7

Schwierigkeitsstufe

Die Begleiter – *der bestimmte und der unbestimmte Artikel*

Was ist das Gegenteil?

1. Finde das Gegenteil der hervorgehobenen Adjektive und setze die richtige Form des unbestimmten Artikels ein.

a **stupid** girl   an *intelligent* girl _____

a **difficult** question   _____

a **boring** lesson   _____

a **nice** boy   _____

a **happy** teacher   _____

a **cheap** pullover   _____

an **ugly** voice   _____

an **old** book   _____

a **terrible** boy   _____

Was weißt du noch?

2. Setze die Formen des unbestimmten Artikels ein und erkläre, wann du *a* oder *an* einsetzen musst.

Das nächste Wort beginnt mit:

_____ girl   _____

_____ bad girl   _____

_____ interesting girl   _____

_____ English girl   _____

_____ uniform   _____

_____ uncle   _____

Test 8

 Schwierigkeitsstufe

Die Begleiter – *der bestimmte und der unbestimmte Artikel*

Die Aussprache von *the*

1. a) Sprich die folgenden Beispielsätze laut aus. Wann musst du den bestimmten Artikel /ðə/, wann /ði/ aussprechen?

   the English lesson   the easy tests

   the boring biology lesson   the exciting exercises

   the teachers at my school   the unhappy pupils

   the difficult questions   the uniforms of English pupils

   the interesting subjects   the old churches

   b) Gibt es beim Gebrauch des bestimmten Artikels Unterschiede zu den Regeln für den Gebrauch von *a/an*?

   _____

   _____

Ken ist krank

2. Ergänze jeweils den richtigen Artikel.

   Today Ken is ill.

   He has got _____ temperature.

   He has got _____ sore throat.

   He has got _____ headache, too.

   Has he got _____ cold?

   Well, I think he has got _____ bad cold, or he has got _____ flu.

   It's _____ pity he can't come to our party.

Test 9

 Schwierigkeitsstufe

Die Begleiter – *der Demonstrativbegleiter*

Mein und dein

1. **Setze die entsprechenden Formen von *this* und *that* ein.**

   _____ is my schoolbag and _____ is your schoolbag.

   _____ is my seat and _____ is your seat.

   _____ is my sandwich and _____ is your sandwich.

   _____ are my books and _____ are your books.

   _____ are my pencils and _____ are your pencils.

   _____ are my CDs and _____ are your CDs.

   _____ is my iPod and _____ is your iPod.

   _____ are my things and _____ are your things.

   _____ is my mobile and _____ is her mobile.

   And _____ is my girlfriend; *don't think she is yours!*

Beim Einkaufsbummel

2. **Ergänze die entsprechenden Formen von *this* und *that*.**

   Look at _____ pullover. It's really nice and _____ pullover is very nice, too.

   Which pullover is nicer, _____ pullover or _____ pullover over there?

   Look! Aren't they lovely? _____ t-shirts right in front of you?

   And what about _____ t-shirts right here?

   I like _____ t-shirts here better. Can we go in and buy one?

   Okay, but let's have a look at _____ shirts in the shop window, too.

Test 10  Schwierigkeitsstufe

Die Begleiter – *der Possessivbegleiter*

Die Formen der Possessivbegleiter

1. **Setze die passenden Possessivbegleiter ein.**

   This is **my** friend. These are _____ friends. (1. Person Plural)

   This is **your** bike. These are _____ bikes. (2. Person Plural)

   This is **his** car. These are _____ cars. (3. Person Plural)

   This is **her** room. These are _____ rooms. (3. Person Plural)

   This is **its** bone. These are _____ bones. (3. Person Plural)

Der Possessivbegleiter *your*

2. **Was kann *your* alles bedeuten? Übersetze.**

   What's *your* telephone number, Mrs Benson? _____

   When is *your* birthday, Tom? _____

   Where is *your* homework, Tom and Ken? _____

   Where's *your* car, Mr and Mrs Benson? _____

   Where's *your* workbook, Alice? _____

Test 11

 Schwierigkeitsstufe

Die Begleiter – *der Possessivbegleiter*

Weitere Verwechslungsmöglichkeiten ...

1. **Da hat doch jemand *its* mit *it's* verwechselt ... Korrigiere den Text. Ersetze *its* durch *it's*, wo *its* falsch ist.**

   Ken goes to a comprehensive school. **Its** a big school. **Its** a new school, too, but not everything is new. **Its** desks are old and a lot of **its** chairs are old, too. But many of **its** teachers are young. Ken likes it there. He thinks **its** a good school and that **its** fun to go there.

Und noch eine weitere Verwechslungsmöglichkeit

2. **Wann ist *their* und wann ist *there* richtig? Setze die entsprechenden Formen ein.**

   Look, that's Tom's house over _____ .

   Where? _____ , on your left.

   That's _____ house? Well, it's a big house.

   Yes, and _____ is a big garden behind it.

   We often play _____ .

   Oh, can we go _____ , too?

Test 12 ▮▮▯ Schwierigkeitsstufe

Das Adjektiv – *das Adjektiv*

Wie sie sein sollen oder wie sie sind ...

1. Wähle unter den folgenden Adjektiven drei aus, die die folgenden Personen charakterisieren.

nice, beautiful, good-looking, clever, crazy, exciting, fat, poor, rich, tall, short, strong, funny, interesting, boring, loud, difficult, old, young , sad, happy, loud, calm, stupid, intelligent, wonderful, uninteresting, aggressive, greedy, nervous, thin, funny

Beispiel: My favourite teacher: *He/she is old and loud, but very funny.*

My English teacher _____

My maths teacher _____

My mother _____

My friend _____

My _____

Welche Adjektive passen?

2. Welche Adjektive verbindest du mit den folgenden Substantiven? Notiere jeweils zwei.

Football? _____

Computers? _____

Boys? _____

Shopping? _____

Comics? _____

Pop stars? _____

Girls? _____

Casting shows? _____

English lessons? _____

Test 13  Schwierigkeitsstufe

Das Adjektiv – *die Steigerung des Adjektivs*

Die Steigerung des Adjektivs

1. Bilde den Komparativ und den Superlativ der folgenden Adjektive.

   rich _____ _____

   cheap _____ _____

   long _____ _____

   loud _____ _____

Achte auf die Schreibung

2. Bilde, wie in Aufgabe 1, den Komparativ und den Superlativ.

   nic**e** _____ _____

   larg**e** _____ _____

   bi**g** _____ _____

   thi**n** _____ _____

   ho**t** _____ _____

   fa**t** _____ _____

Test 14   Schwierigkeitsstufe

Das Adjektiv – *die Steigerung des Adjektivs*

Und nun wird es unregelmäßig ...

1. **Bilde die Steigerungsformen der folgenden Adjektive.**

   good   _____   _____

   bad   _____   _____

   much/many _____   _____

Was ist richtig?

2. **Setze *most* oder *the most* ein.**

   _____ pupils think that homework is useless.

   This is a mistake _____ pupils make.

   _____ mistakes are silly, but this mistake is _____ idiotic.

   Sheila is _____ beautiful girl in our class. _____ pupils like her.

   Ben thinks that _____ girls are stupid.

   He only forgets that he is _____ stupid boy in our class.

Vermischtes ...

3. **Finde die Steigerungsformen der Adjektive.**

   dangerous   _____   _____

   dirty   _____   _____

   interesting _____   _____

   careful   _____   _____

   quick   _____   _____

Test 15  Schwierigkeitsstufe

Das Adjektiv – *die Steigerung des Adjektivs*

Alles zusammengefasst

1. **Ergänze die Lücken entsprechend.**

1. Adjektive mit einer Silbe und Adjektive mit zwei Silben, die auf -*y* und -*le* enden, bilden den Komparativ und den Superlativ mit -*er*, -*est*:

   cold _____ _____

   funny _____ _____

   simple _____ _____

2. Ein stummes -*e* am Ende des Adjektivs entfällt; nach Konsonant wird das *y* zu *i*:

   nice _____ _____

   easy _____ _____

3. Mit ganz wenigen Ausnahmen bilden alle anderen Adjektiven den Komparativ und den Superlativ mit *more*, *the most*:

   expensive _____ _____

   beautiful _____ _____

4. Einige ganz wenige Adjektive haben unregelmäßige Formen:

   good _____ _____

   bad _____ _____

Test 16  Schwierigkeitsstufe

Das Adjektiv – *der Vergleich im Satz*

Vergleiche im Satz

1. **Wähle ein Adjektiv aus und vergleiche. Gebrauche dabei** *as ... as* **oder** *not as ... as.*

   boring   interesting   difficult   bad   intelligent

   football – tennis _____

   swimming – running _____

   English – German _____

   morning lessons – afternoon lessons _____

   books – comics _____

   I – my neighbour _____

   dolls – toy cars _____

Genauso, aber anders ...

2. **Mache die vorige Aufgabe noch einmal, gebrauche aber** *than.*

   _____

   _____

   _____

   _____

   _____

   _____

   _____

Test 17  Schwierigkeitsstufe

Das Adjektiv – *der Vergleich im Satz*

Than, *then* oder *as ... as*?

1. Fülle die Lücken aus. Tipp: Denke dabei daran, dass *then* „dann, damals" heißt. Im Gegensatz dazu entspricht *than* dem deutschen „als" oder „wie" und kann nur im Vergleich gebraucht werden.

I tried to phone you yesterday, but you didn't answer the phone. What were you doing _____? I was reading a book _____. Reading a book? Was it so interesting? More interesting _____ the other one? Yes, it was. What was it about? It was about human intelligence, about the differences between men and women. Are there any? Aren't women _____ intelligent _____ men? Yes, they are. But in some fields men are better _____ women, in some fields they are _____ good _____ women and in some fields they are worse _____ women. Fine, _____ you seem to know everything about this problem ...

Steigerungen sind möglich ...

2. Bilde Sätze mit den folgenden Angaben:

1. Bob / terrible boy / Danny / terrible + / John terrible ++

   Bob is a terrible boy, but Danny is more terrible. John is the most terrible boy of all.

2. This mistake / bad / that mistake + / those mistakes ++

   _____

3. Sue / smart girl / Alice + / Debbie ++

   _____

4. This test / difficult / the English test + / the maths test ++

   _____

5. Bob / noisy / his neighbour + / John ++

   _____

Test 18  Schwierigkeitsstufe

Zusammensetzungen mit no, any, some, every

Fragen und Antworten

1. **Setze die Zusammensetzungen von *any* ein.**

   Does _____ know him? No, nobody knows him.

   Has _____ seen him? No, nobody has seen him.

   Did he go _____ ? No, he went nowhere.

   Can you see him _____ ? No, I can't see him anywhere.

   Did he do _____ ? No, he didn't do anything.

   Did he talk to _____ ? No, he didn't talk to anybody.

Hilfe ...

2. **Setze *jemand*, *etwas* etc. ein.**

   _____ must talk to him.   (jemand)

   We must do _____ about him.   (etwas)

   But what can we do? Can we really do _____ ?   (etwas)

   We must find some help _____.   (irgendwo)

   We must find _____ to help him.   (jemanden)

   If we don't, _____ terrible will happen.   (etwas)

Test 19  Schwierigkeitsstufe

Zusammensetzungen mit no, any, some, every

Was weißt du noch?

1. **Ergänze.**

   Wann musst du *some*, wann *any* gebrauchen? _____

   _____

   Wann musst du *not … any* gebrauchen? _____

   _____

Some und _somebody_ in Fragen

2. **a) Lies diese Sätze genau durch. Welche Antwort wird wohl erwartet?**

   Would you like something to drink?   Do you need some help in the kitchen?

   Can I have some more coffee, please?

   _____

   b) Trage *some* und die entsprechenden Zusammensetzungen ein.

   Can I have _____ money, please? You know, it's time for my pocket money.

   Didn't I give you _____ money yesterday? I really think I did. I hope you have

   got _____ left.

   Let's clean the car. Can _____ come and help me? I really need _____

   help. Well, here's your chance. I'll give you _____ extra money if you help me.

Test 20  Schwierigkeitsstufe

Präpositionen – *Zeitangaben mit Präpositionen*

Es gibt Leute, die gerne arbeiten ...

1. **Setze die richtigen Präpositionen ein.**

   I've got a friend who likes work very much. He works _____ morning _____ night.

   He works _____ the morning, _____ the afternoon, _____ the evening, even

   _____ Saturdays and _____ Sundays. He seldom goes to bed _____

   midnight (vor). He gets up very early, _____ about 6.

   _____ a short breakfast (nach) he settles down to work. Nothing can stop

   him. Last year he even worked _____ his birthday and even _____

   December 25th, Christmas Day. Let's wish him a Merry Christmas this year!

Zeitbezogene Präpositionen

2. **Ergänze die richtigen Präpositionen.**

   Tom was born _____ 1997.

   His birthday is _____ April.

   It is _____ April 2nd. His friend's birthday is _____ the same day.

   It's _____ a Friday this year.

   _____ Saturday they are going to have a big party.

   It's always fun to have parties _____ the weekend!

   It will begin _____ 3 o'clock and end _____ 11.

   They'll prepare for the party _____ morning _____ night (von/bis) on Friday.

Test 21 ■ ■ ☐ Schwierigkeitsstufe

Präpositionen – *Ortsangaben mit Präpositionen*

Dein Zimmer

1. **Beantworte die Fragen. Verwende eine der angegebenen Präpositionen.**

   Where is your bed? _____ (rechts / links / in der Mitte)

   Where are your clothes? _____ (auf / unter / in)

   Where are your posters? _____ (an) the wall.

   Where is your desk? _____ (in der Mitte, links von, rechts von, vor)

   What is _____ your desk?   (auf)

   What is _____ your bed?   (hinter)

Präpositionen, Präpositionen ...

2. **Setze die folgenden Präpositionen ein.**

   near   on   at   to   into   in front of   out of   under   in

   It's already 8 o'clock. Tom's still _____ his room. He's packing his things for school.

   His English textbook is still _____ his desk. Some other books are lying _____

   the floor _____ his bed. His pencil-case is also _____ the desk, _____ his

   computer. He's putting everything _____ his schoolbag. The bus is already wait-

   ing _____ the bus stop. Tom runs _____ the bus stop, but doesn't make it. So

   he has to go _____ school by bike. When he gets there, he rushes _____ the

   classroom, but he's late. His teacher is already there. He's standing _____

   board with the register _____ his hands. A bit late, aren't you, Tom? You couldn't get

   _____ bed this morning, could you?

Test 22  Schwierigkeitsstufe

Präpositionen – *Ortsangaben mit Präpositionen*

Wo sind sie?

1. **Setze die fehlenden Präpositionen ein.**

Where are the children? They are not _____ . They	zu Hause
are not _____ their room.	in
_____ the house there is a field. Are they playing	in der Nähe
_____ the field? It's not very _____ _____ the house.	auf / weit weg von
Or are they _____ the street? There is a garden	auf
_____ the house. Are they there? No, they aren't.	um ... herum
Where are they then? Oh, here they are. They are _____ the	in
living-room. Yes, they are. They are in the living room _____	vor
the telly. What film are they watching? It's a western. Look,	
here it is. It's _____ page 12 of the TV guide.	auf

Was sie bedeuten ...

2. **Ordne die Erklärungen den richtigen Präpositionen zu.**

   1. **to**   a) ist das Gegenteil von *into*

   2. **in**   b) gibt an, dass sich etwas oder jemand auf ein Ziel hinbewegt

   3. **into**   c) ist das Gegenteil von *above* und von *over*

   4. **out of**   d) bedeutet immer *von irgendwo her* oder *weg von*

   5. **from**   e) gibt an, dass jemand oder etwas in einem Raum ist

   6. **at**   f) gibt an, dass jemand oder etwas in einen Raum hineingeht

   7. **on**   g) jemand oder etwas befindet sich auf einer Oberfläche

   8. **under**   h) gibt an, wo jemand oder etwas ist

Test 23 ■■□ Schwierigkeitsstufe

Pronomen – *das Personalpronomen (Subjektfall)*

In der Schule

1. **Setze das richtige Pronomen ein.**

   Hello, _____ am Tom.

   Are _____ new here?

   Where are _____ from?

   What about your parents? Are _____ from Bristol, too?

   Is that your bike? Is _____ new?

   Have _____ got a sister?

   How old is _____ ?

   Is _____ in your class?

   Is _____ nice?

   Can _____ meet her?

Während einer Englischstunde ...

2. **Setze die richtigen Pronomen ein.**

   Where is your homework, Tom?

   _____ is not here. _____ can't find it. _____ must still be on my desk.

   And where is your homework, Danny? Is _____ at home, too?

   No, Sir, _____ think _____ is on the bus.

   What are _____ doing, Alice and Sue? Are _____ doing your homework now?

   No, sir, _____ are just writing a letter.

   What! _____ are writing a letter during the English lesson?

   Yes, Sir, _____ are.

Test 24 ▮▮▯ Schwierigkeitsstufe

Pronomen – *das Personalpronomen (Objektfall)*

Die Formen des Personalpronomens als Objekt

1. Trage die entsprechenden Objektformen des Personalpronomens ein.

   Singular   **Plural**

   I _____ → we _____

   you _____ → you _____

   he _____ → my uncles/they _____

   she _____ → my aunts/they _____

   it _____ → my cats/they _____

Das Pronomen *you*

2. Welche Bedeutung hat *you* in diesen Sätzen?

   a) **You** are right, Tom. _____

   You are right, Tom and Jerry. _____

   You are right, Mr Owen. _____

   You are right, Mr and Mrs Owen. _____

   b) I can't help **you**, Tom. _____

   I can't see **you**, Tom. _____

   I can't help **you**, Tom and Jerry. _____

   I can't see **you**, Mr Owen. _____

   I can't help **you**, Mr. Owen. _____

   I can't see **you**, Mr and Mrs Owen. _____

   I can't help **you**, Mr and Mrs Owen. _____

Test 25

 Schwierigkeitsstufe

Pronomen – *das Personalpronomen (Objektfall)*

Und wie steht es mit den anderen Objektformen?

1. **Wie heißen sie auf Deutsch? Schaue dir die folgenden Sätze an.**

   He can see **me/him/her/it**.   He can see **us/them**.

   He can help **me/him/her/it**.   He can help **us/them**.

   me _____ / _____   us _____ / _____

   him _____ / _____   them _____ / _____

   her _____ / _____

   it _____ / _____

Während der Pause ...

2. **Tom ist wieder auf der Suche. Beantworte Toms Fragen.**

   I can't see ...   *I can't find ...*

   Where is **my schoolbag**? _____

   Where is **my chewing-gum**? _____

   Where are **my sandwiches**? _____

   Where is **my money**? _____

   Where is **Alice**? _____

   Where is **that new boy**? _____

   Where are **the others**? _____

   Where is **my anorak**? _____

   Where are **my glasses**? _____

   Where is **my scarf**? _____

   And where are **my shoes**? _____

Test 26 ▮▮▯ Schwierigkeitsstufe

Pronomen – *das Personalpronomen (Objektfall)*

Was weißt du noch?

1. Übersetze die folgenden Fragen und beantworte dann die Frage zur Grammatik.

   a) Can you help **me**? _____

   b) Can you see **me**? _____

   c) Can you go **with me**? _____

   Wann musst du den Objektfall des Personalpronomens gebrauchen?

   a) für ein Substantiv im _____

   b) für ein Substantiv im _____

   c) für ein Substantiv nach einer _____

Versteckspiel

2. Setze die entsprechenden Pronomen ein.

   Where are Alice and Ken? Everybody is looking for _____ , but nobody can find _____ .
   Where are _____ hiding? The children are looking for Alice first. Where is _____ ? Is
   _____ in Tom's room? No, _____ isn't in the room. _____ is empty. There is no
   trace of* _____ there. Is _____ under Tom's bed? No, _____ isn't. Is _____ behind
   the door? No, _____ isn't. _____ isn't behind _____ . Where is _____ then? _____
   is in the wardrobe, with Ken! _____ are hiding behind some clothes, so nobody can
   find _____ . But _____ are laughing, so the children can hear _____ .

   * There is no trace of ... = Da ist keine Spur von ...

Test 27  Schwierigkeitsstufe

Pronomen – *das Possessivpronomen*

Wie lauten die Formen?

1. Ersetze die Substantive mit dem Possessivbegleiter durch das entsprechende Pronomen.

This is **my pen**.　　　　It's _____ .

Is this **your pen**?　　　Is it _____ ?

That's **her bag**.　　　　That's _____ .

That's **his book**.　　　　That's _____ .

This is **our dog**.　　　　It's _____ .

Is this **your car**?　　　Is this _____ ?

Are these **their bikes**?　Are these _____ ?

In der Schulcafeteria

2. Setze die entsprechenden Possessivpronomen ein.

This is not your table. We are sitting here. This table is _____ .

You sit over there! _____ is over there.

Hey, that's my chair, Ben. It isn't _____ .

Those aren't your seats, Ken und Sam. _____ are over there.

Is this your glass? No, it isn't. It belongs to Alice. It's _____ .

And this plate? Is it yours, Debbie? Yes, it's _____ .

And what about this plate? Is it Tom's? Yes, it is. It's _____ .

Don't eat those chocolate puddings! Mike and Ken put them on the table.

They are _____ .

Is that your purse? I don't think it's _____ . It must be Debbie's.

Yes, it's _____ .

Test 28   ▮▮▯ Schwierigkeitsstufe

Pronomen – *das prop word one*

Shopping

1. **Ersetze die hervorgehobenen Substantive.**

   Look at these pullovers. Do you like them? Which **pullovers**? _____

   The green **pullover** and the blue **pullover** over there. _____

   No, I don't like them, but look at that red **pullover**. I like that one a lot! _____

   I know that red is your favourite colour.

   But why don't you like that **pullover** over there? _____

   You mean the yellow **pullover**? _____

   Yes, that **pullover**. The **pullover** with Big Ben on it. _____

   Okay, it's not too bad.

   Okay, then let's go in and try on that yellow **pullover**. _____

Im Laden

2. **Unterstreiche die Substantive, bei denen das Ersetzen sinnvoll ist.**

   Excuse me, could I try on that yellow pullover?

   Which pullover?

   The pullover over there with Ben Big on it.

   Here you are. Try it on, if you like.

   I like it, but it's a bit too small. Haven't you got a bigger pullover?

   No, I'm afraid not*. That's the only pullover left.

   Okay, could you show me the red pullover over there?

   Sure I can. Just try it on.

   Oh, I like this pullover very much. And how much is it? I'll take it. I love red pullovers.

   * I'm afraid not = Leider nicht

Test 29  Schwierigkeitsstufe

Adverbien – *Bildung und Gebrauch der Adverbien der Art und Weise*

Bildung

1. **Bilde die Adverbien der folgenden Adjektive.**

   bad _____   beautiful _____

   quick _____   complete _____

   nervous _____   noisy _____

   stupid _____   terrible _____

   careful _____   horrible _____

   nice _____   hard _____

   slow _____   lazy _____

   quiet _____   simple _____

   dangerous_____ fast _____

   excited _____   good _____

Wie schreibst du die folgenden Adverbien?

2. **Ergänze die fehlenden Buchstaben.**

   a) awfu____y, crue____y, gratefu____y, officia____y, rea____y, usefu____y

   b) larg____ly, nic____ly, saf____ly, polit____ly, strang____ly, aggressiv____ly

   c) bus____ly, craz____ly, luck____ly, happ____ly, nois____ly

Test 30   Schwierigkeitsstufe

Adverbien – *Steigerungsformen*

I'm the greatest!

1. **Setze das entsprechende Adverb ein.**

   I've got a beautiful voice. I sing _____ .

   I'm a careful driver. I drive _____ .

   I'm a good tennis player. I play tennis _____ .

   I'm a fast swimmer. I swim _____ .

   I'm a hard worker. I work _____ .

   I always give intelligent answers. I always answer questions _____ .

   I'm an excellent dancer. I dance _____ .

Manche können es besser ...

2. **Bilde Sätze mit den folgenden Angaben.**

   Beispiel: John runs fast. Mike +/Ken ++

   John runs fast. Mike runs faster, but Ken runs fastest.

   1) Ken likes Alice very much. Ben +/John ++

   _____

   2) Tom sings well. Bob +/Robert ++

   _____

   3) Mike speaks German badly. John +/Kevin ++

   _____

   4) Sue works hard. Alice +/Kate ++

   _____

Test 31 ▮▮▯ Schwierigkeitsstufe

Adverbien – *der Vergleich im Satz*

Debbie und Tom

1. a) Setze *(not) as ... as* oder *than* und die entsprechenden Formen des Adverbs ein.

   Tom's German is quite good, but he doesn't speak German (1) _____

   Debbie. She speaks German much (2) _____ Tom.

   Tom's voice isn't bad, but Debbie sings (3) _____ Tom.

   Debbie is a fast swimmer, but she doesn't swim (4) _____ he does.

   Debbie is good at sports, but Tom can run (5) _____ she can.

   Both play tennis, but Debbie doesn't play it (6) _____ elegantly _____ Tom.

   Tom is a hard worker, but Debbie works (7) _____ he does.

   b) Wann musst du die Grundform des Adverbs, wann den Komparativ gebrauchen?

   _____

   _____

Und die anderen ...

2. Ergänze, was fehlt.

   a) Mike is a **fast** learner, but there are others who learn _____ he does.

   b) Kevin is a **careful** worker. He works much _____ Mike.

   c) Alice is a **clever** girl, but she doesn't answer _____ Debbie.

   d) Joe's handwriting is **bad**. He writes even* _____ Fiona.

   e) John isn't a **calm** boy. Others do things much _____ he does.

   f) Ken doesn't learn things **easily**. He doesn't learn things _____ Tom.

   * even worse = noch schlimmer; even better = noch besser

Test 32

 Schwierigkeitsstufe

Konjunktionen

Eine Geschichte

1. **a) Lies diese Geschichte und unterstreiche die Konjunktionen, die du in diesem Text findest.**

   A man and his dog are walking along a road. Suddenly the man remembers that he and his dog are already dead. He stops for a moment, but then walks on. After some time they come to a high, white wall. When they get near it, they see a big door in the wall and realize that the street which leads into it is made of pure gold. Then they see a man who is standing there. When they get near enough, they ask him where they are. The man tells them that this place is called heaven.

   b) Welche Aufgaben haben die Konjunktionen in diesem Text?

   _____

Eine kleine Liste

2. **a) Was bedeuten diese Konjunktionen auf Deutsch?**

and _____	if _____/_____
or _____	when _____
but _____	that _____
so _____	so that _____
	because _____
	although _____
	before _____
	until _____

   b) Was verbinden Konjunktionen wie _and_? Was verbinden Konjunktionen wie _if_?

   _____

Test 33 ▮▮☐ Schwierigkeitsstufe

Mengenangaben – *Mengenangaben mit much, many, a lot of, lots of*

Ein Schulfest

1. Setze die entsprechenden Formen von *much / many / a lot of* ein.

   Today there is a big party at Tom's school. _____ people are there. There are _____ pupils of Tom's class, too. There are _____ stalls there, too, where the pupils present their work. There is the photo club, for example. You can see _____ photos at their stall. Then there is the rock club; they play _____ music and have _____ fun. They also have a chess club, where you can meet _____ chess players and play against them. Then there is the bike club. There are _____ bikes at their stall. The pupils there show you how to repair your bike, so _____ pupils visit their stall.

Fragen

2. a) Setze *much / many / a lot of / lots of* richtig ein.

   How _____ is this bike? It costs too _____ money!

   How _____ bikes have you got here?

   How _____ bikes can you repair in a day?

   How _____ money does it cost to repair a bike?

   Are there any girls in the club, too? How _____ girls are in your club?

   How _____ time do spend there? I spend so _____ time there!

   How _____ pupils are in the club?

   b) Wann kannst du *much* und *many* nicht durch *a lot of* ersetzen?

   _____

Test 34 ▮▮▯ Schwierigkeitsstufe

Mengenangaben – *weitere Mengenwörter*

Sag es anders

1. **Ersetze *no* durch *not ... any*.**

Mike has got
- no friends. _____
- no money. _____
- no parents. _____
- no brothers and sisters. _____
- no family. _____
- no food at home. _____
- no fun. _____

Gehen wir ins Kino!?

2. **Setze die passenden Mengenwörter ein.**

Is there _____ good film on tonight?

Yes, there is. There's a good film in the Rex.

Okay, let's go there. Oh, but there's a problem. I haven't got _____ money on me.

I hope you have got _____.

Sorry, I haven't. I haven't got _____ money on me either.

What can we do then? Have you got _____ ideas?

Let me think. Oh yes, let's ring up Alice. Perhaps she has got _____ money and

can lend us _____. Perhaps she can even come with us.

But Alice has got _____ time and _____ money. She must do some

babysitting because her parents are out. Poor Tom and Ken! They're not having

_____ luck tonight!

Test 35 ■■□ Schwierigkeitsstufe

Mengenangaben – *weitere Mengenwörter*

Sam

1. Setze die folgenden Begleiter so ein, dass der Text einen Sinn ergibt. Bei manchen Sätzen hast du mehrere Möglichkeiten.

   many   a few   some   any   a little   much

   Sam is still a small boy. He can speak, but _____ of his sentences are not correct. He makes _____ mistakes. You need _____ time to understand him. His real problem, however, is food. He only likes _____ things. _____ vegetables are a real horror to him and he doesn't eat _____ meat. He also doesn't drink _____ milk. What he likes, are sweets, but too _____ sweets aren't good for him.

Zusammenfassung und Übersicht

2. Fülle die Tabelle richtig aus.

deutsche Bedeutung	Substantiv im Singular	Substantiv im Plural
viel(e)		
wenig(e)		
ein paar / einige		
ein bisschen		
etwas		
kein(e)		

Test 36

 **Schwierigkeitsstufe**

Mengenangaben – *Mengenangaben mit dem of-Genitiv*

Mengenangaben mit dem *of*-Genitiv

1. Verbinde die folgenden Mengenangaben mit einem passenden Substantiv.

a cup	of	shoes
a glass	of	bread
a bowl	of	cake
a plate	of	names
a piece	of	soup
a bag	of	lemonade
a slice	of	peas
a bar	of	chocolate
a tin	of	crisps*
a box	of	coffee
a bottle	of	butter
a pound	of	milk
a pair	of	oranges
a list	of	sausages

   * crisps = Kartoffelchips (AmE: chips)

Hier stimmt was nicht

2. Korrigiere, was falsch ist. Verwende dabei andere Mengenangaben.

a box of water	_____	a pound of milk	_____
a glass of apples	_____	a slice of toast	_____
a tin of crisps	_____	a box of cornflakes	_____
a piece of tea	_____	a bottle of chocolate	_____

Test 37

Schwierigkeitsstufe

Mengenangaben – *Mengenangaben mit Zahlen*

Mengenangaben mit Zahlen

1. Stelle die Fragen und beantworte sie. Beginne mit *there is / there are ...* Schreibe insgesamt 7 Sätze.

   Beispiel: *There are thirty-two pupils in my classroom.*

How many	boys	are there		
	girls			
	desks		in your school?	
	pupils		in your class?	
	teachers		in your classroom?	
	windows			
	posters			

Auch Schüler sind vergesslich ...

2. Am Endes des Schuljahres werden die Sachen ausgelegt, die die Schüler während des Jahres vergessen haben ... Schreibe auf, was sie liegen gelassen haben.

There are / There is	15 pairs of trainers	in the caretaker's room.	
	2 right shoes		
	7 left shoes		
	4 shirts		
	6 anoraks		
	1 schoolbag		
	8 socks		
	5 English textbooks		

Test 38  **Schwierigkeitsstufe**

Zahlen und Daten – *Kardinalzahlen*

Zahlenreihen

1. Lies die folgenden Zahlen laut. Welche Zahlen passen nicht zu den anderen? Schreibe sie auf.

   a) 7   14   21   29   35   _____

   b) 9   18   27   37   45   _____

   c) 99   90   81   75   63   _____

   d) 77   71   63   56   49   _____

   e) 63   60   58   54   51   _____

   f) 12   18   25   30   36   _____

Hier wird es schwieriger ...

2. Lies die folgenden Zahlen laut und schreibe sie aus.

3	13	33
4	14	44
5	15	55
8	18	88
9	19	99

Test 39 Schwierigkeitsstufe

Zahlen und Daten – *Uhrzeit, größere Zahlen und Jahreszahlen*

Die Uhrzeit

1. *What time is it?* Schreibe die folgenden Uhrzeitangaben aus.

6.00 _____ 9.35 _____

6.30 _____ 10.20 _____

6.45 _____ 10.30 _____

7.15 _____ 11.40 _____

8.50 _____ 11.55 _____

Toms Stundenplan für Montag

2. Schreibe den Stundenplan aus.

8.50 – 9.40	9.45 – 10.35	10.35 – 10.50	10.55 – 11.45
English	PE	break	Maths
11.50 – 12.40	12.40 – 13.40	13.45 – 14.30	14.35 – 15.25
Geography	lunch	Music	Art

Tom's first lesson is from _____ to _____ .

PE is from _____ to _____ .

Break is from _____ to _____ .

Maths is from _____ to _____ .

Geography is from _____ to _____ .

Lunch break is from _____ to _____ .

Music is from _____ to _____ .

Test 40  Schwierigkeitsstufe

Zahlen und Daten – *Uhrzeit, größere Zahlen und Jahreszahlen*

Große Zahlen ...

1. Schreibe die folgenden Zahlen aus.

   100 _____

   200 _____

   345 _____

   888 _____

   1,000 _____

   2,000 _____

   100,000 _____

   1,000,000 _____

Jahreszahlen

2. Weißt du noch, wie man Jahreszahlen liest? Es ist ganz einfach:

   1492 *fourteen (hundred and) ninety-two*   1900 *nineteen hundred*

   1648 *sixteen (hundred and) forty-eight*   2001 *two thousand one*

   Lies und schreibe die folgenden Daten aus:

   1776 _____

   2008 _____

   1888 _____

   1066 _____

   1668 _____

   1096 _____

   2049 _____

Test 41   ■ □ □   Schwierigkeitsstufe

Zahlen und Daten – *Ordnungszahlen, Wochentage und Monatsnamen*

Ordnungszahlen

1. Lies die folgenden Ordnungszahlen laut und schreibe sie aus.

1st the _____   12th _____

2nd the _____   14th _____

3rd _____   15th _____

4th _____   19th _____

5th _____   20th _____

8th _____   31st _____

9th _____   44th _____

11th _____   67th _____

Ein Quiz

2. Beantworte die Fragen.

Which is the second month of the year? _____

What about December? Which month is it? _____

When is Christmas in English-speaking countries? On the _____ of December.

And which is the fifth month? _____

Which is the eighth month? _____

And what about Tuesday? Which day of the week is it? _____

Which is the fifth day of the week? _____

Which is the first day of the week? _____

Look at Tom's timetable. Which lesson is Art? _____

And which lesson is Maths? _____

Test 42 ■■□ Schwierigkeitsstufe

Zahlen und Daten – *Ordnungszahlen, Wochentage und Monatsnamen*

Was sind das für Wochentage und Monatsnamen?

1. **Schreibe sie richtig.**

   senadydwe _____

   yrefabur _____

   robetoc _____

   thydrusa _____

   omnyda _____

   yuanajr _____

   tugsua _____

   syatruda _____

   amcrh _____

   ysetuda _____

Geburtstags-Tage!

2. **An welchem Wochentag ist Toms Geburtstag dieses Jahr?**

   It's on a F _____ .

   And when is his father's? It's on a W _____ .

   And when is his mother's? It's on a Tu _____ .

   And when is his cousin's? It's on a Sa _____ .

   And when is his friend's? It's on a Th _____ .

   And when is Debbie's birthday? It's on a Su _____ .

   And when is your birthday this year? It's on _____ .

Test 43

 **Schwierigkeitsstufe**

Zahlen und Daten – *Daten und Feiertage*

Daten

1. **Lies und schreibe die folgenden Daten aus.**

   17/12/1956

   _____

   28/06/1940

   _____

   25/07/2008

   _____

   19/04/1913

   _____

   03/12/2001

   _____

Öffentliche Feiertage in Great Britain

2. **Kannst du die Feiertage den Daten zuordnen? Schreibe auf, was du gefunden hast.**

New Year's Day	Boxing Day	Christmas Day	May Day	Summer Bank Holiday
27/08	1/5	1/1	25/12	26/12

New Year's Day is _____

Boxing Day is _____

Christmas Day is _____

May Day is _____

Summer Bank Holiday is _____

Test 44  | Schwierigkeitsstufe |

Das Präsens von to be – *bejahte und verneinte Formen von to be*

Dannys Fragen

1. **Danny ist total durcheinander. Stelle seine Fragen.**

    you / Excuse me / Tom / are? _____ ?

    you / are / from Bristol? _____ ?

    that / your sister / is? _____ ?

    she / in your class / is? _____ ?

    what / her name / is? _____ ?

    how / is / she / old? _____ ?

    these boys / in your class / are / too? _____ ?

    your classroom / is / that? _____ ?

    the man over there / a teacher / is? _____ ?

Fragen über Fragen

2. **Gib Kurzantworten.**

    a) Are you often late? No, _____ .

    b) Are your teachers always late? No, _____ .

    c) Are your friends happy? Yes, _____ .

    d) Are you and your friends happy? Yes, _____ .

    e) Are you a nice and friendly person? Yes, _____ .

    f) Are you a good pupil? Yes, _____ .

    g) Are your marks always good? Yes, _____ .

    h) Is this exercise difficult? No, _____ .

    i) And your school reports? Are they good? Yes, of course _____ !

Test 45

☐☐☐ Schwierigkeitsstufe

Das Präsens von to be – *there is/there are und Fragen mit that*

Deine Schule

1. **Gib Kurzantworten auf Fragen mit** *there is / there are.*

   Are there many pupils at your school? _____

   Are there many boys in your class? _____

   Are there any nice girls/boys in your class? _____

   Is there a cafeteria at your school? _____

   Is there a gym, too? _____

   Is there an outdoor swimming pool, too? _____

   Are there many activities at your school? _____

   Is there a theatre group or a photo club? _____

Fragen mit *that*

2. **Gib Kurzantworten.**

   Is that an English book? Yes, _____.

   Is that an interesting book? No, _____.

   Is that your teacher? Yes, _____.

   Is that Mr Mason? Yes, _____.

   Is that your school? No, _____.

   Is that your boyfriend? Yes, _____.

   Is that your girlfriend? No, _____.

   Is that a silly question? Yes, _____.

Test 46 ▣▣☐ Schwierigkeitsstufe

Das Präsens von to be – *Fragen und Kurzantworten*

Fragen mit Fragewörtern

1. **Stelle Fragen mit den Fragewörter *who, how, what, where*.**

   _____ are you?   I'm Tom.

   _____ are you?   Fine, thanks. And you?

   _____ is his name?   His name is Ken.

   _____ is your friend?   Danny is my friend.

   _____ old are you?   I'm twelve.

   _____ are the other boys?   They are at school.

   _____ is your bike?   It's right there.

   _____ is your sister?   She's at home.

   _____ is your English teacher?   Mr Mason is my English teacher.

   _____ is that on your chair?   It's a book.

   _____ kind of book is it?   It's an English book.

Und nun auf Deutsch!

2. **Übersetze die folgenden Sätze!**

   Wo bist du? _____

   Wie heißt du? _____

   Wo bist du her? _____

   Wie heißt dein Vater? _____

   Wie alt bist du? _____

   Wo sind deine Eltern? _____

   Wer ist dein Freund? _____

Test 47 Schwierigkeitsstufe

Das Präsens von have got – *bejahte und verneinte Formen von have got*

Nicht jeder hat alles ...

1. Schreibe auf, was sie haben und was nicht.

Sam	Ken	The Bensons	Emma	Alice
~~brother~~	~~sister~~	~~flat~~	bike	mobile
aunt	brother	house	~~car~~	~~computer~~

Sam _____ a brother, but _____ an aunt.

Ken _____, but _____ .

The Bensons _____. They _____ .

Emma _____. She _____ .

Alice _____, but she _____ .

Ich möchte alles wissen ...

2. Stelle Fragen und antworte.

a) _____ you _____ a sister, Sam?

No, I _____ a sister, but I _____ an aunt.

b) _____ you _____ a sister, Ken?

No, I _____ a sister, but _____ a brother.

c) _____ a flat, Mr and Mrs Benson?

No, we _____ a flat. We _____ a house.

d) _____ Emma _____ a bike?

Yes, _____ a bike, but she _____

a car.

Test 48  Schwierigkeitsstufe

Das Präsens von have got – *Fragen und Antworten mit have got und to be*

Deine Schule

1. **Gib Kurzantworten mit *to be* und *have got*.**

   Is your school a big school? _____

   Are there many pupils in your class? _____

   Have you got any friends in your class? _____

   Have you got a boyfriend/girlfriend? _____

   What about your teachers? Are they nice? _____

   Have your teachers got time for you? _____

   Have you got many lessons in the afternoon? _____

   Are you happy with your school reports? _____

   Are your parents happy with your school reports? _____

   Are you nervous before a test? _____

   Is English your favourite subject? _____

Pass auf die Schreibung auf!

2. **Wo muss, wo darf kein *e* stehen?**

   My parents **hav__n't** got a flat. They **hav__** got a house.

   Our house **is____n't** a big house, but it is big enough for us.

   The rooms **ar__n't** very big, and the garden is small, too.

   But I **hav____** got my own room, and my sister **has__** got her own room, too.

   We **ar____** very happy about that. We **hav____** got enough room for our things.

Test 49  Schwierigkeitsstufe

Das Präsens der Hilfsverben – *can* und *may*

Can und *may*

1. a) **Setze die entsprechenden Formen von *can* und *may* ein.**

   I _____ speak English, but I _____ speak Spanish.

   _____ we see each other tomorrow, Alice? No, I _____ . I'm busy.

   _____ I smoke here, sir? No, you _____ .

   _____ I do my homework here? Yes, you _____ .

   b) **Wo liegen die Unterschiede zwischen *can* und *may*?**

   _____

   _____

Eine Frage in der Not?

2. **Setze die Formen von *can* und *may* ein.**

   _____ I ask you a question, sir?

   Yes, you _____ .

   _____ I leave the classroom, sir?

   Okay, but first tell me why you want to leave.

   I must go to the toilet, sir. _____ I leave the classroom now?

   John, just have a look at your watch. _____ you tell me the time?

   Yes, I _____ . It's three minutes to twelve.

   Well, John, then you certainly _____ wait another three minutes.

   Oh sir, I hope I _____ .

Test 50  Schwierigkeitsstufe

Das Präsens der Hilfsverben – *can, must, needn't und mustn't*

Was kann ich für dich tun?

1. **Übersetze die folgenden Sätze. Gib auf die Wortstellung acht!**

   Was kann ich für dich tun? _____ ?

   Wie kann ich dir helfen? _____ ?

   Warum kannst du mir nicht helfen? _____ ?

   Was musst du tun? _____ ?

   Wohin musst du gehen? _____ ?

Eine Klage

2. **Korrigiere die Wortstellung.**

   I / always do / must / what others tell me. _____ ?

   Get up early / must / I. _____ ?

   I / the bus / mustn't / miss. _____ ?

   My homework / do / I / must. _____ ?

   I / at school / stay / must / all day long. _____ ?

Test 51 █ █ ☐ | Schwierigkeitsstufe

Das Präsens der Hilfsverben – *can, must, needn't und mustn't*

Was musst du machen, wenn du krank bist?

1. Stelle dir vor, du wärst krank und müsstest zuhause bleiben. Was dürftest du und was nicht? Setze die richtigen Hilfsverben ein (müssen, dürfen, brauchen).

I _____ stay in bed.   I _____ take my medicine.

I _____ do my homework. I _____ go to school.

I _____ play football.   I _____ see a doctor

Was musst, kannst, darfst du (nicht) an der Schule tun?

2. Setze die richtigen Hilfsverben ein. Es gibt mehrere Möglichkeiten.

I _____ clean the classroom.   I _____ call my teacher names.

I _____ kiss my teacher.   I _____ listen to my teacher.

I _____ talk to my neighbour. I _____ do my homework.

I _____ smoke at school.   I _____ fight with my neighbour.

Test 52   ■ ☐ ☐   Schwierigkeitsstufe

Der Imperativ

Aufforderungen

1. Übersetze diese Sätze.

   Come here, Tom. _____

   Come here, Tom and Mike. _____

   Come here, Mr Benson. _____

   Come over to our place, Mrs Benson. _____

   Come with us, Mr and Mrs Benson. _____

Was du so zu Hause hörst ...

2. **Welche Verben könntest du hier einsetzen?**

   C _____ back soon.

   B _____ here at seven.

   P _____ up your socks.

   E _____ your soup.

   T _____ up your room.

   H _____ a bath or a shower.

   W _____ your hands.

   B _____ your teeth.

   D _____ your homework.

   H _____ me now.

   S _____ the table.

   D _____ the dishes.

   G _____ to bed now.

Test 53    Schwierigkeitsstufe

Das present progressive – *das Partizip Präsens*

Die regelmäßige Bildung des Partizip Präsens

1. Bilde das Partizip Präsens der folgenden Verben.

clean_____   wash _____   sing _____

laugh _____   talk _____   fight _____

drink _____   eat _____   listen _____

shout _____   knock _____   do _____

watch _____   fix _____   go _____

buy _____   play _____   say _____

cry _____   try _____   carry _____

Etwas weniger regelmäßige Formen ...

2. Beachte die Bildung des Partizip Präsens bei den folgenden Verben.

write _____   choose _____   lose _____

come _____   ride _____   take _____

change _____   have _____   drive _____

trip _____   plan _____   put _____

sit _____   clap _____   run _____

drop _____   stop _____   swim _____

cut _____   get _____   forget _____

lie _____   die _____   tie _____

Test 54 Schwierigkeitsstufe

Das present progressive – *present progressive*

In der Pause

1. **Was machen die Kinder gerade im Pausenhof? Bilde Sätze mit den folgenden Angaben.**

   They/eat their sandwiches _____

   Many/stand together in groups _____

   They/talk _____

   Somebody/shout _____

   Some children/play _____

   Two pupils/fight _____

   Somebody/call a teacher _____

Nach der Pause

2. **Bilde Sätze im *present progressive*.**

   The pupils/leave the schoolyard. _____

   They/go into the school building. _____

   Some/run. _____

   A pupil/lie/on the floor. _____

   He/cry. _____

   A teacher/come. _____

   The teacher/carry him into the office. _____

   He put/him on a stretcher*. _____

   The secretary/get him a glass of water. _____

   She/call an ambulance. _____

   * stretcher = Bahre

Test 55

Schwierigkeitsstufe

Das present progressive – *Fragen und Antworten im present progressive*

Der Lehrer kommt ...

1. **Was tun sie gerade? Bilde Fragen.**

Tom / sit / in * his chair? _____?

He / do / an exercise? _____?

Kevin and Ken / make / girls angry? _____?

Alice / flirt / with Mike? _____?

Robert / lie / on the floor? _____?

Bob, Ben and John / play / cards? _____?

Debbie / read / a magazine? _____?

Fiona / run / around the classroom? _____?

Tim / play / football in the classroom? _____?

* Man kann sowohl *to sit in a chair* als auch *to sit on a chair* sagen. Beides ist richtig.

Ja oder nein?

2. **Schaue dir die vorige Aufgabe noch einmal an und gib dann Kurzantworten.**

Is Debbie reading a magazine? Yes, _____.

Is Robert running around the classroom? No, _____.

Are Kevin and Ken doing exercises? No, _____.

Is Alice flirting with Tom? No, _____.

Are Fiona and Tom playing cards? No, _____.

Is Tom doing his exercises? Yes, _____.

Is Ben lying on the floor? No, _____.

Is Debbie crying? No, _____.

Are Kevin and Ken playing with the girls? No, _____.

Is Tim drawing a picture? No, _____.

Test 56

 Schwierigkeitsstufe

Das present progressive –
Verben mit Präpositionen im present progressive

Verben mit Präpositionen

1. Füge die entsprechende Präposition hinzu.

What are you looking _____ ?	(suchen)
Who are you waiting _____ ?	(warten)
Who are you looking _____ ?	(ansehen)
What are you listening _____ ?	(zuhören)
What are you talking _____ ?	(reden über)
Who are you looking _____ ?	(sich kümmern um)
Who are you thinking _____ ?	(denken an)
Why are you running _____ ?	(wegrennen)
What are you writing _____ ?	(aufschreiben)
What word are you looking _____ ?	(nachschlagen)
What are you putting _____ your bag?	(hineintun)
What trousers are you trying _____ ?	(anprobieren)

Was ist das Gegenteil?

2. Setze die richtige Präposition ein.

to get on a bus	to get _____ a bus
to turn a radio on	to turn it _____
to put on a shirt	to take it _____
to take off your clothes	to put them _____
to fall asleep	to wake _____
to stand up	to sit _____

Test 57  Schwierigkeitsstufe

Das simple present – *simple present*

Ein typischer Abend bei den Bensons

1. Setze die richtigen Verbformen ein.

   When the Bensons _____ home, it's still very early.   (come)

   Then they _____ tea.   (have)

   After tea, they _____ up the dishes.   (wash)

   Tom sometimes _____ them.   (help)

   Then Mrs Benson _____ his newspaper.   (read)

   Mrs Benson _____ a magazine or a book.   (read)

   Later they _____ TV.   (watch)

   Mr Benson _____ films. His wife _____ so, too.   (like / do)

   At about eleven they _____ to bed.   (go)

Und was tun sie *nicht* am Wochende?

2. Gebrauche die verneinten Formen des *simple present*.

   The Bensons / not get up / early.   They _____ .

   Mrs Benson / not go / to work.   She _____ .

   They / not have / an early breakfast.   They _____ .

   They / not make / their beds.   They _____ .

   Tom / not do / any homework.   He _____ .

   He / not go / to school.   He _____ .

   Mr Benson / not do / the gardening.   He _____ .

   The Bensons / not stay / at home all day.   They _____ .

Test 58

 | Schwierigkeitsstufe |

Das simple present – *simple present*

Einige Fragewörter

1. Mit welchen Fragewörtern fragst du nach dem Subjekt, Objekt usw.?
   Trage sie in die Tabelle ein.

Debbie	sees	Tom	in the classroom	at 9.
The shop	shows	its top cars	in its showrooms	this week.
Subjekt	**Verb**	**Objekt**	**Ort**	**Zeit**
a) _____		a) _____		
b) _____	_____	b) _____	_____	_____

Fragen im *simple present*

2. Frage nach dem Subjekt, dem Verb, dem Objekt, dem Ort und der Zeit in den oben stehenden Sätzen.

   a) Subjekt: _____

   _____

   b) Verb: _____

   _____

   c) Objekt: _____

   _____

   d) Ort: _____

   _____

   e) Zeit: _____

   _____

Test 59 ■ ■ ☐ Schwierigkeitsstufe

Das simple present – *Fragen mit Fragewörtern im simple present*

Die Fragebildung

1. **Schaue dir die Fragen in Aufgabe 2 aus dem vorigen Test noch einmal genau an und vergleiche sie mit der Lösung. Beantworte dann die folgenden Fragen.**

   a) Wann musst du *what*, wann *who* gebrauchen?

   what: ☐ Sachen   ☐ Personen   ☐ Zeiten

   who: ☐ Sachen   ☐ Personen   ☐ Orte

   b) Welches Fragewort musst du gebrauchen, wenn du nach dem Verb fragst?

   ☐ how   ☐ who   ☐ when   ☐ why   ☐ what   ☐ where

   c) Wann gebrauchst du *to do* bei der Fragebildung nicht?

   ☐ in Fragen nach dem Objekt   ☐ in Fragen nach dem Verb

   ☐ in positiven Fragen nach dem Subjekt

   d) Bei einer Frage nach dem Subjekt steht das Verb im Plural oder im Singular?

   Kleiner Tipp: Im Deutschen ist es genauso!

   ☐ im Singular   ☐ im Plural

Mr Hedges

2. **Stelle jeweils zwei Fragen nach den hervorgehobenen Satzteilen.**

   Mr Hedges works as a caretaker **at Tom's school**.

   _____?

   _____?

   He likes **his job**.

   _____?

   _____?

   Children like **him**.

   _____?

   _____?

Test 60 　■■■ Schwierigkeitsstufe

Das simple present – *Fragen mit Fragewörtern im simple present*

Weitere Fragewörter

1. **Setze *how, why, which, what* ein.**

   _____ many books do you read a year? About 50 books, I think.

   _____ often do you go to the public library? Once a week.

   _____ don't you buy them? They are too expensive.

   _____ much does this book cost? It costs £ 10.

   _____ book are you talking about? The green book over there.

   _____ do you read so many books? I like books.

   _____ kind of books do you like? I like all kinds of books.

Du und das Fernsehen

2. **Übersetze die folgenden Fragen.**

   Magst du Fernsehen? _____

   Was schaust du normalerweise im Fernsehen an? _____

   Was für Filme magst du? _____

   Was sagen deine Eltern dazu? _____

   Welche anderen Programme schaust du dir an? _____

   Wie oft machst du das Fernsehen an? _____

   Wie lange schaust du fern? _____

   Wann machst du das Fernsehen aus? _____

   Schläfst* du manchmal vor dem Fernseher ein? _____

   Wann gehst du ins Bett? _____

   * to fall asleep = einschlafen

Test 61

 | Schwierigkeitsstufe |

simple present und present progressive – *Gebrauch des simple present*

Wie sieht es bei den Bensons aus?

1. **Schreibe, wie der Tag bei den Bensons verläuft. Gebrauche die folgenden Angaben. Die Verben und Signalwörter musst du allerdings ergänzen.**

   get up at seven / wash / dress / breakfast / leave the house at 8 / Mrs Benson bus /

   work in a hospital / look after patients / lunch there, too / Mr Benson work for a

   newspaper / write and correct articles / often Mr Benson lunch in town / the Bensons

   home in the early evening / tea or supper

   _____

   _____

   _____

   _____

   _____

Und was tun sie am Abend?

2. **Übersetze die hervorgehobenen Signalwörter für das *simple present*.**

   They **often** play with their children. _____

   They **always** talk to them. _____

   They **often** help them with their homework. _____

   They **usually** watch TV or read a book. _____

   They **sometimes** go out. _____

   They **never** stay out all night. _____

   Sometimes their friends come to see them. _____

   They **always** have a good time. _____

   They are **seldom** bored. _____

   They **never** get angry. _____

Test 62

 Schwierigkeitsstufe

simple present und present progressive – *Gebrauch des simple present*

Ein richtiger Engel

1. Beantworte die folgenden Fragen mit einer Kurzantwort und Signalwörtern wie *never*, *always* etc.

   1. Do you often drive your teachers crazy? (No / never)

      _____

   2. Are you always a friendly person? (Yes / seldom unfriendly)

      _____

   3. Are you always happy when you go to school? (Yes / always)

      _____

   4. Do your teachers give you good marks*? (Yes / usually)

      _____

   5. Do you listen to your teachers? (Yes / always)

      _____

   * marks (AmE: grades) = Noten (Schule)

Und was tust du sonst noch?

2. Schreibe auf, was du tust. Verwende die folgenden Angaben und Signalwörter:

   play computer games with my friends   get older   get a birthday present

   get pocket money from my parents   brush my teeth

   Every morning I _____.

   Every afternoon I _____.

   Every day I _____.

   Every week I _____.

   Every year I _____.

Test 63

 | Schwierigkeitsstufe

simple present und present progressive –
Gebrauch des present progressive

Und was geschieht gerade jetzt?

1. a) Bilde Sätze mit den angegebenen Verben.

The sun _____. (shine)

It's not _____. (rain)

The birds _____. (sing)

And we _____ indoors! (sit)

We _____ a test*. (do)

Look! Mike _____. (dream)

He _____ to the birds. (listen)

Our teacher _____ to talk to Mike. (try)

b) Erkläre, warum du hier das *present progressive* gebrauchen musst.

_____

_____

* einen Test schreiben = to do a test (AmE: to take a test)

Signalwörter

2. Welche Signalwörter kannst du nicht mit dem *present progressive* gebrauchen?

next year	listen!	this morning	then
at this moment	just	this afternoon	today
look!	now	this evening	the next day
every morning	after that	the next evening	seldom

Test 64  Schwierigkeitsstufe

simple present und present progressive –
simple present oder present progressive?

Ein armes Mädchen

1. Welche der hervorgehobenen Verben kannst du normalerweise nicht im *present progressive* verwenden? Unterstreiche sie.

   Everybody **knows** me, but nobody **understands** me.

   Nobody **comes** to see me. Nobody **talks** to me. I **am** all alone.

   Nobody **likes** me, nobody **wants me** and nobody **loves** me. I **cry** all day.

   Can you **hear** me? Can you **see** me?

Ein „böses" Mädchen

2. *Present progressive* oder *simple present*?

   Alice often _____ TV, but this evening she _____ to watch anything. (watch/not want)

   She _____ to go out. Today _____ her girlfriend's birthday, and there will be a party at her house. (want/be)

   Alice _____ to be there, but her mother _____ her friends. (want/not like)

   She _____ why Alice _____ such friends. (not understand/have)

   What can Alice do? Look! She _____ (be) in her room.

   She _____ in front of the mirror. She _____ on her new dress and a bit of make-up! (stand/put)

   What _____ she _____?! (do) She _____ out. (go)

   _____ she always _____ things like that? (do)

   Yes. She always _____ what she wants! (do)

Test 65 ▢▢▢ Schwierigkeitsstufe

Vergangenheit von to be und das past progressive –
simple past von to be

Fragen an Tom

1. **Setze die Formen des *simple past* von *to be* ein und gib Kurzantworten.**

   a) _____ you ill, Tom? Yes, _____ .

   b) _____ you worried? No, _____ .

   c) _____ your parents worried? Yes, _____ .

   d) _____ your friends there? Yes, _____ .

   e) _____ all of them there? No, _____ .

   f) _____ Alice there? No, _____ .

   g) _____ Debbie there? Yes, _____ .

   h) _____ she rude to you? No, _____ .

   i) _____ you happy? Yes, _____ .

Weitere Fragen an Tom

2. **Stelle Fragen mit Fragewörtern. Ergänze die fehlenden Formen von *to be*.**

   Why/not at school last week? _____ ?

   How long/ill? _____ ?

   Why/ill? _____ ?

   When/better again? _____ ?

   How many of your friends/there? _____ ?

   Who/missing? _____ ?

   Why/Debbie not there? _____ ?

   Where/the doctor? _____ ?

Test 66 ▪▪▫ Schwierigkeitsstufe

Vergangenheit von to be und das past progressive – *past progressive*

Gestern um 7 Uhr ...

1. **Bilde Sätze mit dem *past progressive*.**

   When the doorbell rang yesterday morning at seven o'clock, ...

   I/just get up _____

   my parents/have breakfast _____

   my father/read morning paper _____

   my sister/still sleep _____

   our neighbors/still lie in their beds _____

   my younger brother/still dream _____

   other people/have a good time _____

Gestern um 11 Uhr morgens

2. **Bilde Sätze im *past progressive* mit den folgenden Angaben.**

   Yesterday at 11 am ...

   most people/not lie in their beds anymore _____

   my parents/not have breakfast anymore _____

   most people/not sleep anymore _____

   I/not lie in my bed anymore either _____

   I/not sit at the breakfast table anymore _____

   I not play/football _____

   I/sit on a chair _____

   I/do an English test* _____

   * to do a test (AmE: to take a test) = einen Test schreiben

Test 67  Schwierigkeitsstufe

Das simple past – regelmäßige Verben im simple past

Das *simple past* der Vollverben

1. **Bilde das *simple past* der folgenden Verben.**

   a) happen, knock, pass, push; _____

       turn, watch, cheer, cook, talk; _____

       answer, ask, climb, finish; _____

       explain, guess, help, look; _____

       stay, play, enjoy _____

   b) love, dance, explore, agree _____

   c) invite, hate, point, end, fold _____

   d) hurry, cry, carry, tidy _____

   e) plan, drop, stop, clap _____

Was weißt du noch?

2. **Ergänze den Text.**

   1. Bei Verben, die das *simple past* regelmäßig bilden, wird ein _____ an den Infinitiv angehängt.
   Wo bereits ein -e vorhanden ist, entfällt dieses (z. B.: *dance* + *ed* = *danced*).

   2. Die Endung -ed wird bei Verben, die auf ein gesprochenes / t / oder / d / enden, wie _____ ausgesprochen (z. B. *hate* + *ed* = *hated*).

   3. Ein -y wird nach _____ zu *ie*; nach _____ bleibt es erhalten (z. B. *try* → *tried*, aber *play* → *played*).

   4. Der letzte Konsonant bei einsilbigen Verben mit kurzem betonten Vokal wird _____ (z. B. *drop* → *dropped*).

Test 68 ▮▮☐ Schwierigkeitsstufe

Das simple past – *unregelmäßige Verben im simple past*

Unregelmäßige Formen

1. **Bilde das** *simple past* **der folgenden Verben.**

choose _____	eat _____	speak _____
come _____	fly _____	stand _____
do _____	fall _____	take _____
drive _____	feel _____	tell _____
keep _____	leave _____	throw _____
lose _____	make _____	know _____
meet _____	read _____	write _____
have _____	go _____	wear _____
hear _____	give _____	fight _____
hurt _____	hide _____	mean _____
sell _____	ride _____	find _____

Welches Verb passt nicht?

2. **Bilde das** *simple past* **der folgenden Verben. Ein Verb passt jedoch nicht in die jeweilige Reihe. Unterstreiche es!**

1. cut _____	get _____	put _____	cost _____
2. know _____	fly _____	grow _____	show _____
3. drink _____	sing _____	begin _____	win _____
4. sleep _____	keep _____	feel _____	see _____
5. catch _____	think _____	bring _____	buy _____

Test 69 ▉▉☐ Schwierigkeitsstufe

Das simple past – *Gebrauch und Verneinung im simple past*

Ein schlauer Bursche

1. Setze die verneinten Vergangenheitsformen ein.

   The police examined the rooms,

   but they _____ anything.   (not find)

   There _____ any finger prints.   (not be)

   They _____ any tools.   (not see)

   There _____ any shoe prints on the floor.   (not be)

   The burglar _____ an amateur.   (not be)

   He _____ many mistakes.   (not make)

   He _____ the police to catch him.   (not want)

   The police _____ happy.   (not be)

Weißt du noch ...?

2. Wie bildest du die Verneinung im *simple past*? Fülle die Lücken aus.

   a) Du bildest die Verneinung mit _____ oder _____ (Kurzform).

   b) Danach folgt immer der _____ .

   c) Bei *to be* steht keine Form von *to* _____ . Hier genügt ein _____ .

   d) Verneine die folgenden Sätze.

they saw	_____	they noticed	_____
they found	_____	they heard	_____
they listened	_____	this meant	_____
I understood	_____	they were	_____
I did	_____	we did	_____

Test 70  Schwierigkeitsstufe

Das simple past – *Fragen und Antworten im simple past*

Kein Verhör, aber Fragen

1. **Stelle die Fragen der Polizisten.**

   a) You call us half an hour ago? _____ ?

   b) You leave the window open? _____ ?

   c) Anybody know that you were out tonight? _____ ?

   d) You turn the lights on? _____ ?

   e) You notice anything out of the ordinary*? _____ ?

   f) Your neighbour notice** anything? _____ ?

   g) You be out all evening? _____ ?

   h) You shut that door? _____ ?

   i) The burglar*** steal anything? _____ ?

   j) He open that safe? _____ ?

   * anything out of the ordinary = irgendwas Außergewöhnliches
   ** to notice = erkennen, mitbekommen
   *** burglar = Einbrecher, Dieb

Was die Masons antworteten

2. **Schaue dir die Fragen in der vorigen Aufgabe noch einmal an. Gib dann die entsprechenden Kurzantworten.**

   a) Yes, _____ .   f) No, _____ .

   b) No, _____ .   g) Yes, _____ .

   c) No, nobody _____ .   h) No, _____ .

   d) Yes, _____ .   i) Yes, _____ .

   e) Yes, _____ .   j) Yes, _____ .

Test 71   ◼◼☐ Schwierigkeitsstufe

Das simple past – *Fragen und Antworten im simple past*

Was weißt du noch?

1. **Beantworte die folgenden Fragen.**

   1. Mit welchen Fragewörtern fragst du nach dem Subjekt und dem Objekt?

      ☐ who   ☐ why   ☐ what   ☐ how

   2. Bei welchen Fragen darfst du *to do* nicht gebrauchen? _____

      _____

   3. Und wie ist es bei Fragen nach anderen Satzteilen? Was musst du dann gebrauchen?

      _____

      _____

Weitere Fragen

2. **Stelle Fragen nach den markierten Substantiven.**

   The burglar broke into the house.

   _____

   The neighbours didn't see **him**.

   _____

   The burglar opened **the safe**.

   _____

   The burglar took the money out of the safe.

   _____

   The burglar took **the money** out of the safe.

   _____

Test 72    Schwierigkeitsstufe

simple past und past progressive – *Gebrauch des past progressive*

Im Schwimmbad

1. **Bilde das *past progressive* mit den folgenden Angaben (Achtung, einmal geht es nicht!).**

   Yesterday Tom and some others went to the swimming pool. When they arrived ...

   the sun / shine _____

   the sun / not hide behind clouds _____

   many people / be / there _____

   many people / swim in the pool _____

   others / talk to their friends _____

   others / play football _____

   some people / sleep _____

   some / read a book or a magazine _____

   some / lie in the sun and dream _____

Ein ruhiger Nachmittag

2. **Setze die Formen des *past progressive* ein.**

   Everything was peaceful.

   People not shout _____

   People not run around _____

   People not fight _____

   Mike lie peacefully in the grass _____

   Ken not scream at the others _____

   Only John tell silly stories _____

Test 73 ▉▉☐ Schwierigkeitsstufe

simple past und past progressive – *Gebrauch des simple past*

Ein Ausflug Teil I

1. **Gestern besuchte Toms Klasse den Zoo von Bristol. Hier ist Toms Bericht. Setze die Verben in das *simple past*.**

   Yesterday we _____ to the zoo with Mr Winterbottom, our biology teacher (go).

   We _____ to the bus stop (walk). We _____ on the bus (get).

   In the bus we _____ for our seats (look). Everybody _____

   happy (be). But soon the trouble _____ (start). Mike _____

   (not feel) very well. He _____ sick (get). It _____ terrible (be)!

Ein Ausflug Teil II

2. **Hier ist einiges durcheinandergeraten. Bringe die Sätze in die richtige Reihenfolge und setze die Verben in das *simple past*.**

   ☐ The bus _____ at the zoo. (arrive)

   ☐ He _____ angry. (become)

   ☐ Some pupils _____ to run around inside the bus. (start)

   ☐ Others _____ to eat their crisps. (begin)

   ☐ The bus driver _____ this. (see)

   ☐ He _____ to shout. (begin)

   ☐ There _____ crisps everywhere. (be)

   ☐ We _____ off the bus. (get)

   ☐ I _____ happy. (be)

   ☐ We _____ there. (be)

   ☐ Other pupils _____ their feet on the seats. (put)

Test 74 ▪▪▪ Schwierigkeitsstufe

simple past und past progressive – *simple past oder past progressive?*

Ein Unfall

1. **Füge die richtigen Verbformen ein.**

Suddenly the bus _____ to a stop (come). John _____ still _____ (stand), and he _____ (fall) onto the floor and _____ (hit) his head on a seat. One of the pupils _____ Mr Winterbottom at once (call). He _____ very angry (become) when he _____ (see) that John _____ (lie) on the floor. "Why don't you listen?" he _____ (shout). But when he _____ (see) that John's mouth _____ (bleed), he _____ (run) to the bus driver and _____ (ask) him to call a doctor. A few minutes later an ambulance _____ (arrive). Two paramedics* _____ (come) into the bus. They _____ (have) a look at the boy. Then they _____ (fetch) a stretcher. They _____ (put) John on it and _____ (load**) him onto the ambulance.

* paramedic (ambulance man) = Sanitäter, Rettungsassistent, Notarzt
** to load = befördern

In der Notaufnahme Teil I

2. **Es waren viele Leute in der Notaufnahme. Einige unterhielten sich und erzählten, weshalb sie hier waren. Setze die richtigen Verbformen der folgenden Verben ein.**

I _____ a shower when I _____ . (have / slip)

I _____ the windows when one window _____ , and the broken glass _____ my hands. (clean / break / cut)

And what did John tell them? _____

_____

Test 75 ■■■ Schwierigkeitsstufe

Die Vergangenheit der Hilfsverben – can, may, must, need

In der Notaufnahme Teil II

1. Unterstreiche im Text die Hilfsverben. Setze dann den ganzen Text in das *simple past*.

The paramedics take John to the accident and emergency department*. He must wait for a doctor. He feels better, but he can't move. So he can only stay where he is. He can't walk around the room. When the nurse comes in, she tells him that he must stay where he is and that he mustn't stand up. But she also tells him that he needn't worry.

_____

_____

_____

_____

* Notaufnahme = accident and emergency department, A&E (AmE = emergency room, ER)

Wie lauten ihre Vergangenheitsformen?

2. Ergänze die Vergangenheitsform. Sieh dir dann die Lösungen an und korrigiere, was du eventuell falsch gemacht hast.

can	_____	(konnte)
can't	_____	(konnte nicht)
can/may	_____	(durfte)
can't/may not	_____	(durfte nicht)
mustn't	_____	(durfte nicht)
needn't	_____	(musste nicht, brauchte nicht)

Lerne dann diese Vergangenheitsformen auswendig!

Test 76

Schwierigkeitsstufe

Die Vergangenheit der Hilfsverben – *can, may, must, need*

Was dann geschah

1. Setze die entsprechenden Vergangenheitsformen ein! Pass dabei auf, ob diesen Formen ein *to* folgt!

John _____ go home.	(durfte)
He _____ stay in hospital.	(musste nicht)
He _____ go to school.	(brauchte nicht)
He _____ stay in bed for three days.	(musste)
His friends _____ come to see him, ...	(konnten)
but they _____ stay more than half an hour.	(durften nicht)
After 30 minutes, they _____ to leave.	(mussten)

Besorgte Fragen

2. Stelle John die folgenden Fragen.

you / go home?	_____	(durftest)
you / stay in hospital?	_____	(musstest nicht)
you / go to school?	_____	(brauchtest nicht)
you / stay in bed?	_____	(musstest)
you / watch TV?	_____	(durftest)
your friends / visit you?	_____	(durften)
they / stay with you?	_____	(durften)
they / talk with you?	_____	(konnten)
When they / leave?	_____	(mussten)

Test 77  Schwierigkeitsstufe

Einige Besonderheiten – *shall und should*

Wie kann ich helfen?

1. **Mache Vorschläge mit *shall*.**

   buy a sandwich for you / do it for you / keep you company / carry it for you /
   find a place for you to sleep / explain it to you

   "My schoolbag is so heavy." _____

   "I'm so tired." _____

   "I'm so hungry." _____

   "I can't do my homework." _____

   "This exercise is so difficult." _____

   "I am so lonely." _____

Was kann man tun?

2. **Gib Ratschläge mit *should* (= sollte). Welche Sätze passen zusammen?**

   a) "I'm so tired."   not eat so much

   b) "My tests are so bad."   study* harder

   c) "TV is boring."   ask her out on a date

   d) "My jeans don't fit anymore."   look for them

   e) "I'm getting so fat."   not stay up so late

   f) "My skirt is so dirty."   go home now

   g) "My room is a real mess."   wash it

   h) "I've lost my keys."   tidy it up

   i) "Alice likes me."   not watch so much TV

   j) "My parents are waiting for me."   buy new ones

   * to study = studieren, lernen/pauken

Test 78  Schwierigkeitsstufe

Einige Besonderheiten – *to want to, I'd like to, could*

Could

1. **Schaue dir die folgenden Sätze genau an und beantworte dann die Fragen.**

   Could you help me, please?

   Could you come at three o'clock?

   Could your sister come, too?

   When we have finished, we could go for a walk.

   Or we could have a drink somewhere.

   a) Was bedeutet *could* in diesen Sätzen? Was kann *could* noch bedeuten?

   _____   _____

   b) Worum handelt es sich bei diesen Sätzen? Was drücken sie aus?

   _____   _____

Tea time

2. **Übersetze die folgenden Sätze.**

   Möchtest du noch etwas Zucker?

   _____

   Könntest du mir ein Stück Kuchen geben?

   _____

   Willst du noch etwas Milch?

   _____

   Ich will nicht nach Hause gehen.

   _____

Test 79 ◼◼☐ Schwierigkeitsstufe

Einige Besonderheiten – *have got und to have*

Ein armer Mann

1. **Gebrauche das Vollverb *to have* für *have got*.**

   Mr Fletcher hasn't got anything. _____

   He hasn't got a house. _____

   He hasn't got a wife. _____

   He hasn't got a family. _____

   He hasn't got a job. _____

   He hasn't got any money. _____

   He hasn't got a car. _____

   He hasn't got any friends. _____

   He hasn't got anything. _____

Einmal anders gefragt ...

2. **Stelle dieselben Fragen mit *to have*.**

   Have your parents got a house? _____

   Has Debbie got a hamster? _____

   Have her parents got a cat? _____

   Have you got a problem? _____

   Has Mike got a bike? _____

   Have these people got the tickets? _____

   Has this girl got a friend? _____

   Have you got a lot of courage? _____

Test 80  Schwierigkeitsstufe

Einige Besonderheiten – *Ausdrücke mit to have*

Badezimmerprobleme

1. *Have got* oder *have*? Wo kannst du *have got* nicht einsetzen?

   It's early in the morning. The children are getting up for school. They always _____ an argument before they decide who can go to the bathroom first. The reason is that Alice always needs such a long time in the bathroom. First she _____ a shower, and then she washes her hair. After that she _____ a chat with her dolls. She keeps her dolls in the bathroom, and Alice _____ many of them. So when Alice goes to the bathroom first, the others _____ very little time to use it. They can't _____ a shower or a bath. They can only wash their faces, brush their teeth and then – maybe – they have time to _____ a very quick breakfast. Then they rush off to school on their bikes.

Ein genauerer Blick ...

2. **Welche Formen von *have/have got* musst du einsetzen?**

   Alice, can we come in now? No, you can't, I _____ a shower.
   Come on, Alice, hurry up! We want to _____ a shower, too.
   Just go and _____ your breakfast. You can _____ a shower after that.
   Five minutes later they come back, but Alice is still in the bathroom. She _____ a chat with her dolls now. They _____ the day off, so they _____ a lot of time. So there is no need to _____ an argument today!

Test 81  Schwierigkeitsstufe

Einige Besonderheiten – *must und to have to*

Auch deine Eltern müssen Dinge tun ...

1. Bilde 4 Sätze mit den folgenden Angaben.

   Beispiel: *They had to clean their car though they didn't want to.*

   pay the bills _____

   clean the flat _____

   go to work _____

   listen to me _____

Must und *to have to*

2. a) Lies den Text durch und finde die richtige Bedeutung der zwei folgenden Sätze:
   Müssen kann im Englischen mit *to have to* und mit *must* übersetzt werden. Allerdings werden beide Ausdrücke unterschiedlich verwendet. Das Verb *to have to* drückt ein Müssen aus, das von außen / von jemand anderem kommt. (Beispiel: *I have to work.* Denn, wenn ich nicht arbeite, verdiene ich kein Geld zum Leben.) Bei *must* ist das Müssen dagegen oft ein innerer Zwang. (Beispiel: *I really must go now.* Denn ich möchte meine Freunde nicht warten lassen.)

   1. I must see you.   a) My mother told me to see you.

   2. I have to see you.   b) I really love you and can't live without you.

   Im *simple past* gibt es diesen Unterschied allerdings nicht mehr. Hier heißt es immer "I had to" = „Ich musste".

   I _____ see you.

   b) Setze *must* oder *have to* ein.

   1. I really _____ go now. My parents are waiting for me.

   2. Where is Debbie? I _____ see her. I can't live without her.

   3. I am afraid I can't come this afternoon. My mother told me I _____ do my homework first.

   4. I _____ learn English. I need it for my job.

Test 82  Schwierigkeitsstufe

present perfect und simple past – *past participle*

Das *past participle* – regelmäßige Bildung

1. Wie du weißt, wird das *present perfect* mit den Formen von *have* und dem Partizip der Vergangenheit gebildet. Die Formen von *have* kennst du, aber weißt du auch noch, wie das Partizip gebildet wird? Bilde das *past participle* von den folgenden Verben:

talk	_____	dance	_____
end	_____	play	_____
try	_____	return	_____
carry	_____	kill	_____
drop	_____	stop	_____
look	_____	die	_____
tie	_____	paint	_____

    Erinnern dich diese Formen an etwas? Richtig: Sie werden genauso gebildet wie die regelmäßigen Formen des _____ .

Unregelmäßige Partizipien

2. Wie lauten die *past participles* der folgenden Verben?

be	_____	have	_____
choose	_____	lose	_____
fly	_____	know	_____
feel	_____	fall	_____
write	_____	think	_____
go	_____	do	_____
say	_____	tell	_____
wear	_____	buy	_____

Test 83

 Schwierigkeitsstufe

present perfect und simple past – *present perfect*

Ein bewegter Tag

1. **Bilde Sätze im *present perfect* mit den folgenden Angaben.**

   Tom / be / to school. _____

   He / just / come back. _____

   His mum / be / shopping. _____

   She / buy a lot of things. _____

   She / do / the cooking. _____

   She / clean the bathroom. _____

   Tom / help her. _____

   They / have a busy day. _____

   They / do / a lot of things. _____

Toms Vater

2. **a) Bilde Sätze im *present perfect*.**

   Tom's father / be / very busy, too. _____

   He / leave the house. _____

   But he / not be in his office. _____

   He / not help his wife. _____

   He / be away on business. _____

   He / take the train to London. _____

   b) Wo stehen im *present perfect* die Ergänzungen zum Verb?

   ☐ vor dem Partizip   ☐ hinter dem Partizip

Test 84  Schwierigkeitsstufe

present perfect und simple past – *Signalwörter für das present perfect*

In einem Reisebüro

1. **Lies dir den folgenden Text durch und gib Kurzantworten.**

   Good afternoon. Have a seat, please. What can I do for you? *We'd like to book a holiday, but we haven't decided yet. I hope you can help us.* Okay, then let me ask you some questions first.

Have you ever been to Italy?	No, _____.
Have you been to Spain yet?	No, _____.
Haven't you been to Majorca yet?	No, _____.
Have you already been to Wales?	No, _____.
Have you always spent your holidays in GB?	Yes, _____.
Have you never been abroad*?	No, _____.

   Okay, then have a look at this catalogue, please. It has just arrived.

   * abroad = im Ausland

Signalwörter

2. **Lies den letzten Kurztest erneut durch und schreibe die Signalwörter heraus, die mit dem *present perfect* stehen.**

   a) Was bedeuten sie auf Deutsch und b) wo stehen sie im Satz?

   Signalwörter   deutsche Bedeutung

   e _____   _____

   y _____   _____

   n _____ y _____   _____

   a _____   _____

   a _____   _____

   n _____   _____

   j _____   _____

   b) yet: _____   ever, never, already: _____

Test 85

 Schwierigkeitsstufe

present perfect und simple past – *Gebrauch des present perfect*

Was ich noch weiß

1. **Schaue dir die Sätze genau an und beantworte dann die folgenden Fragen.**

   The Bensons will spend their holidays in Wales.

   They have never been there. They have always spent their holidays in England.

   Their tickets have just arrived. They have just opened the envelope.

   a) Was für Handlungen drückt das *present perfect* aus? Wann haben sie begonnen?
   Wann sind sie vorbei?

   _____

   b) Wie sieht es aus mit Handlungen, bei denen *just* (= gerade) steht?
   Wann sind sie zu Ende gegangen?

   _____

Was sie schon getan haben

2. **Setze die folgenden Sätze in das *present perfect*.**

   1. They/buy a map. _____

   2. They/plan their route. _____

   3. They/clean their car. _____

   4. They/prepare some sandwiches. _____

   5. They/buy something to drink. _____

   6. They/pack their bags. _____

   7. They/have put their bags in the car. _____

   8. They/lock the door. _____

   9. They/leave a window open. _____

Test 86 ▪▪▪ Schwierigkeitsstufe

present perfect und simple past – *present perfect oder simple past?*

Hunger

1. **Das *present perfect* oder das *simple past*? Setze die richtigen Zeiten ein.**

   Tom: I'm really hungry. You know we _____ (not stop) once the whole way, and we _____ (leave) this morning at about 8 o'clock.

   Tom's father: I'm very hungry, too. I _____ (not eat) anything either.

   Tom's mother: I _____ (have) a sandwich this morning, but you _____ (not want) to eat any of them. At least, that's what you _____ (say) this morning. I _____ (have) two sandwiches, so I'm not that hungry.

Im Restaurant

2. **Setze die richtigen Zeiten ein.**

   Tom's father: Waiter, can we have the menu, please?

   Waiter: Here you are. I'm afraid, we don't have any fresh fish today. The weather _____ (be) so bad this morning that the fisherman _____ (cannot) go out and fish. In fact, the fishermen _____ (not catch) any fish all week.

   Tom's father: Have you got any sausages? What about eggs and peas?

   Waiter: Sorry, we are out of everything. Nobody _____ (go) shopping this morning.

   Tom's father: What kind of restaurant is this? With no food? Okay, then let's go to our hotel and eat Mum's old sandwiches. I hope you _____ already _____ (not throw) them away.

Test 87  Schwierigkeitsstufe

will-future und going to-future – *will-future*

Und wie wird das Wetter?

1. **a) Setze die entsprechenden Formen des *will-future* ein.**

   Tomorrow the weather _____ better (be).

   There _____ (not be) any rain in the morning.

   There _____ (be) a lot of sunshine in the afternoon.

   But in the evening it _____ cloudy (be).

   There _____ (be) rain in some parts of the country.

   Temperatures _____ (be) around 20 °C in the afternoon.

   b) Wovon hängen diese Handlungen bzw. Zustände ab?

   Von dem, was die Bensons wollen oder wünschen oder von äußeren Bedingungen,

   die sie nicht beeinflussen können?

   _____

Und was glauben die Bensons?

2. **a) Bilde Sätze im *will-future* mit den folgenden Angaben.**

   I think/it be pretty good today.   _____

   Probably/it be warmer later.   _____

   Probably/it not rain.   _____

   I hope/there not be a storm again.   _____

   I believe/it be rather windy, though*. _____

   * though – jedoch

   b) Was drücken Verben wie *I believe*, *I hope*, *I'm sure* aus?

   _____

Test 88  Schwierigkeitsstufe

will-future und going to-future –
will-future in if-clauses und Sätzen mit when

Zusammenfassung

1. Ordne die Beispielsätze den passenden „Regeln" für das *will-future* zu.

Das *will-future* gebraucht man

_____ 1) The weather will be nice tomorrow.

a) um Vermutungen und Hoffnungen auszudrücken.

_____ 2) If the weather is nice tomorrow, we will go to the beach.

b) für zukünftige Handlungen und Ereignisse, die nicht vom Wollen des Sprechers abhängen.

_____ 3) I think it will be warmer later.

c) in Nebensätzen der Zeit und der Bedingung, wenn sie sich auf die Zukunft beziehen.

When und if

2. a) Bei welchen Sätzen ist die Handlung sicher oder wahrscheinlich?

1) When Tom comes, he will help you.   2) If Tom comes, he will help you.

When bezieht sich auf einen Zeitpunkt, zu dem etwas geschieht oder geschehen wird (*when* = wenn). *If* drückt dagegen eine Annahme oder Möglichkeit aus (*if* = falls).

b) Setze *when* oder *if* ein.

1) What will the Bensons do _____ there is another tornado?

(Tornados sind selten.)

2) What will Tom do _____ he gets home?

(Tom wird in 2 Stunden nach Hause kommen.)

3) What will he do _____ there is no more food?

(Es ist Samstag, 20 Uhr und der Supermarkt ist fast leer gekauft.)

4) Will Tom be happy _____ he sees his friend again?

(Seine Freundin wird am nächsten Tag aus dem Urlaub zurückkommen.)

Test 89   Schwierigkeitsstufe

will-future und going to-future – *Gebrauch des going to-future*

Fragen an dich

1. **Bilde die Fragen und gib Kurzantworten.**

   1) You / work harder this term?

      _____ ? _____ , _____ .

   2) You / study more for your tests?

      _____ ? _____ , _____ .

   3) You / get better marks*?

      _____ ? _____ , _____ .

   4) You / watch less TV?

      _____ ? _____ , _____ .

   5) Your friends / help you?

      _____ ? _____ , _____ .

   * marks (AmE: grades) = Schulnoten (NICHT "notes"! Falsche Freunde!)

Fragen mit Fragewörtern

2. **Bilde fünf sinnvolle Fragen mit den folgenden Substantiven, Pronomen und Verben:**

   Subjects: your parents, Debbie, you, your friends, Alice, Tom, he

   Verbs: buy, call, come, see, do, meet, visit

   What _____ ?

   Why _____ ?

   When _____ ?

   Who _____ ?

   Where _____ ?

Test 90  Schwierigkeitsstufe

will-future und going to-future – *going to-future oder will-future?*

Was weißt du noch?

1. Das *going to-future* bezieht sich auf die Zukunft; es wird für zukünftige feste Pläne und Absichten gebraucht.
   Das *will-future* wird gebraucht,
   a) wenn man ausdrücken will, dass etwas unabhängig vom eigenen Wollen in der Zukunft geschieht;
   b) für Hoffnungen und Vermutungen;
   c) im Hauptsatz, wenn der Nebensatz eine Bedingung oder eine Annahme enthält, die sich auf die Zukunft bezieht.

   1) I think he will be there, but I'm not sure.   ☐ richtig   ☐ falsch

   2) We're going to be there tomorrow. I promise!   ☐ richtig   ☐ falsch

   3) I don't care what he says! I am going to watch TV tonight.   ☐ richtig   ☐ falsch

Debbies Geburtstagsparty

2. **Setze das *going to-* oder das *will-future* ein. Vergiss nicht das *to*!**

   a) This year Debbie _____ be twelve.

   b) She _____ have a big party.

   c) She _____ invite all her friends.

   d) She is sure that her parents _____ let her have the party.

   e) She hopes that all her friends _____ come.

   f) She hopes that it _____ not rain.

   g) If it doesn't rain, they _____ be able to play in the garden.

   h) She doesn't know yet when everyone _____ arrive.

   i) She _____ buy some lemonade, some coke and a lot of crisps*.

   j) She _____ get* some sausages and some ice-cream, too.

   k) She believes that everybody _____ like that.

   * crisps (AmE: chips) = Kartoffelchips (Tipp: Im Britischen heißt ˝chips˝ Pommes!)
   ** to get = holen (nicht nur „bekommen˝)

Test 91

 Schwierigkeitsstufe

Die Zeitenbildung im Überblick – *Zeitenbildung*

Ein Überblick

1. **Setze die Verben in die entsprechenden Zeiten.**

   a) Debbie _____ back. (be – present)

   b) She _____ back. (just come – present perfect)

   c) She _____ little time. (have got – present)

   d) She _____ her things. (unpack – pres. progressive)

   e) She _____ go to school on Monday. (have to – present)

   f) She _____ in Majorca with Mum. (be – past)

   g) She _____ go with her. (must – past)

   h) She _____ stay home. (mustn't – past)

   i) But she _____ her stay anyway. (enjoy – past)

   j) She _____ on the beach. (can lie – past)

   k) They _____ there again. (go – going to-future)

   l) The next time _____ fun, too! (be – will-future)

Was entspricht wem?

2. **Welche Zeiten entsprechen diesen Bildungsregeln? Trage sie ein.**

   Subjekt + be + present participle = _____

   S + have + past participle = _____

   S + infinitive + (e)s in der 3. Person sing. = _____

   S + infinitive + -ed / irreg. form = _____

   S + will + infinitive = _____

   S + be + going to + infinitive = _____

Test 92   ■■□ Schwierigkeitsstufe

Die Zeitenbildung im Überblick –
Fragen nach dem Subjekt und anderen Satzteilen

Fragen nach dem Subjekt

1. **Stelle Fragen nach dem Subjekt.**

   The Wilsons have come back. _____ ?

   Debbie has gone to school again. _____ ?

   Her mother doesn't feel well. _____ ?

   Debbie feels sad. _____ ?

   Debbie and her mother aren't happy. _____ ?

   Their holidays are over. _____ ?

   Mrs Wilson enjoyed the holidays. _____ ?

   Mrs Wilson didn't want to come back. _____ ?

   Debbie's books are lying on the floor. _____ ?

   Debbie is going to go there again. _____ ?

Das solltest du jetzt wissen …

2. **Suche die richtige Antwort heraus. Manchmal sind mehrere Antworten richtig.**

   a) Bei Fragen nach dem Subjekt gebrauchst du: ☐ what   ☐ who   ☐ how

   b) Das folgende Verb steht danach immer im: ☐ Singular   ☐ Plural

   c) Bei Fragen nach dem Subjekt darfst du im *simple present* oder im *simple past to do*

   nur in: ☐ verneinten   ☐ nicht verneinten   Fragen gebrauchen.

   d) Bei Fragen nach allen anderen Satzteilen steht im *simple present* und *simple past*

   immer die entsprechende Form von: ☐ to be   ☐ to do

Test 93  Schwierigkeitsstufe

Die Zeitenbildung im Überblick –
Fragen nach dem Subjekt und anderen Satzteilen

Aber es gibt auch gute Dinge ...

1. **Frage nach den hervorgehobenen Satzteilen.**

   She can see **her friends** again. _____ ?

   They are waiting for her. _____ ?

   She will see them **in a few days**. _____ ?

   They are going to talk about **their holidays**. _____ ?

   She can see **Tom**. _____ ?

   She likes **him**. _____ ?

   She knows **that he likes her**. _____ ?

   They can **play tennis** together. _____ ?

Frag Debbie

2. **Gib Kurzantworten.**

   1) Did you enjoy your holidays? Yes, _____ .

   2) Where were you? Were you in Majorca? Yes, _____ .

   3) Are you unhappy now? No, _____ .

   4) Do you feel sad? Yes, _____ .

   5) Do you want to go to school again? No, _____ .

   6) Have you already packed your things? No, _____ .

   7) Can I come to see you? Yes, _____ .

   8) Have you seen Tom yet? No, _____ .

   9) Are you going to see him tomorrow? Yes, _____ .

   10) Will that make you happy? Yes, _____ .

Test 94    Schwierigkeitsstufe

Die Wortstellung – *die Stellung des Subjekts im Aussagesatz*

Vor dem Wiedersehen

1. **Wie lauten diese Sätze richtig?**

   a) Yesterday/didn't/Debbie/feel well.

   _____

   b) But today/feels better/Debbie.

   _____

   c) Tom/she/can see/today/again.

   _____

   d) At 8.30/is going to/at school/be/she.

   _____

   e) So/will have/they/enough time/to see each other.

   _____

Was werden sie tun?

2. **Bilde 5 Sätze mit den folgenden Angaben. Beginne mit dem Nebensatz.**

   When they see each other

   not cry   not talk about school   laugh a lot   have fun together   be happy

   When they _____

   _____

   _____

   _____

   _____

Test 95 ▉▉☐ Schwierigkeitsstufe

Die Wortstellung – *die Stellung des Subjekts im Fragesatz*

Bald geht es wieder los ...

1. **Stelle Fragen.**

   The children are back. _____?

   Two children are ill. _____?

   They can't come. _____?

   They caught a cold yesterday. _____?

   The teachers are there, too. _____?

   Lessons will begin soon. _____?

   A teacher is coming. _____?

   The classroom door opens. _____?

   The pupils stand up. _____?

Wo steht das Subjekt bei Fragen?

2. **Markiere jeweils die richtige Aussage.**

   1) Bei dem *present* und *past* von *to be* steht das Subjekt

      ☐ a) vor den Formen von *to be*.　　☐ b) nach den Formen von *to be*.

   2) Bei einem Prädikat, das aus zwei Teilen besteht (z. B. *will be*) steht das Subjekt

      ☐ a) nach dem ersten Teil des Prädikats.　　☐ b) am Satzanfang.

   3) Dies gilt auch bei Fragen nach dem Subjekt.

      ☐ a) richtig　　　　　　　　☐ b) falsch

   4) Bei Fragen nach dem Subjekt ist die Wortstellung: *Who/what* + Verb.

      ☐ a) richtig　　　　　　　　☐ b) falsch

Test 96  Schwierigkeitsstufe

Die Wortstellung – *die Stellung des Objekts*

Wo ist Tom?

1. a) Übersetze die folgenden Sätze.

   Hast du **Tom** gesehen?

   _____

   Ich kann **ihn** nicht finden.

   _____

   Ja, ich habe **ihn** gesehen.

   _____

   Als ich ihn sah, hat er **Debbie** gesucht.

   _____

   Er hat auch **eine CD** gesucht.

   _____

   b) Wo steht im Englischen das Objekt? Wo steht es im Deutschen?

   _____

   _____

German English ...

2. **Wie lauten die Sätze richtig?**

   I have him just seen.   _____

   He will to Debbie's house again go.   _____

   He will the house again leave.   _____

   He has something forgotten.   _____

   He must for it look.   _____

   He will it find.   _____

Test 97

Schwierigkeitsstufe

Die Wortstellung – *die Stellung von Orts- und Zeitangaben*

Toms Freizeitkalender

1. Schreibe auf, was Tom tun will.

Monday	clean my bike	On Monday, he's going to clean his bike.
Tuesday	study for a test	
Wednesday	play table tennis	
Thursday	see Debbie	
Friday	practice playing the guitar	
Saturday	watch a football match on TV	
Sunday	go to the cinema with Debbie	

Deine Pläne

2. a) Sage, was du tun willst. Gebrauche dabei die folgenden Zeitangaben:

tonight   on Monday   next week   this summer   in July   this school year

_____   (learn French)

_____   (stay in bed)

_____   (go to a pop concert)

_____   (work more)

_____   (go on holidays)

_____   (go to Spain)

b) Wo stehen Zeitangaben im Englischen? Sie stehen entweder am

_____ oder _____ .

Test 98  Schwierigkeitsstufe

Die Wortstellung – *die Stellung von Orts- und Zeitangaben*

Ortsangaben

1. a) Unterstreiche die Ortsangaben und bilde Sätze.

   There / near Tom's school / a park / is. _____

   He / there / often / goes. _____

   It's not very far. He / can / there / walk. _____

   There's / in the park / a playground. _____

   They / can / in the park / play. _____

   b) Wo stehen Ortsangaben zumeist im Englischen? _____

   c) Wo können sie sonst noch stehen? _____

Das englische Schulsystem

2. a) Bilde Sätze mit den folgenden Angaben.

   1) pupils / start school / when they are five / in England

   _____

   2) to a comprehensive school / most English pupils / when they are eleven / go

   _____

   3) they / can / when they are 16 / leave school

   _____

   4) in most schools / at 8.30 / lessons start

   _____

   b) Wenn in einem Satz Orts- und Zeitangaben zusammentreffen, wie ist dann die Reihenfolge? _____

Test 99   ▥▥☐ Schwierigkeitsstufe

Die Wortstellung – *die Stellung der Adverbien*

Gibt es solche Schüler?

1. **Setze die entsprechenden Adverbien der Häufigkeit ein.**

   They are loud (often). _____

   They run around (always). _____

   They have learned to sit still (never). _____

   They listen (never). _____

   They forget their homework (usually). _____

   Have you met such people (ever)? _____

   They drive their teachers crazy (sometimes). _____

Adverbien der Art und Weise

2. **Übersetze folgende Sätze.**

   a) „Ich muss gehen", sagte er ruhig.

   _____

   b) Er machte langsam die Tür zu.

   _____

   c) Er schloss die Tür sorgfältig ab.

   _____

   d) Dann öffnete er schnell seine Tasche.

   _____

   e) Er steckte schnell den Schlüssel hinein.

   _____

Test 100  Schwierigkeitsstufe

Notwendige Relativsätze – *die Relativpronomen who, which, whose*

Ein Mädchen

1. **Setze** *who, which* **oder** *whose* **ein.**

   a) Do you remember the girl _____ photo I showed you yesterday?

   b) That's the girl _____ father is a teacher.

   c) Yesterday she was in the bus _____ stops near our house.

   d) She was reading the book _____ we talked about yesterday.

   e) She's somebody _____ can really drive you crazy.

   f) She's a girl _____ thinks she knows everything.

   g) She is somebody _____ thinks that she is more intelligent than others.

   h) That's something _____ is very difficult for me to understand.

Debbie and Tom

2. **Setze die Relativpronomen nur dann ein, wenn du sie einsetzen musst.**

   a) Do you know the photo _____ I gave to John? The one over there?

   b) That's a photo of Debbie. You know? The girl _____ Tom likes so much?

   c) She lives in a place _____ isn't very far from his street.

   d) She is the most intelligent girl _____ he knows.

   e) That's the girl _____ maths tests are better than his.

   f) She's good at sports, too. Hockey is the game _____ she is best at.

   g) And she's good-looking. Tom thinks she is the most beautiful girl _____ he has ever seen.

Test 101  Schwierigkeitsstufe

Notwendige Relativsätze – *Relativsätze mit und ohne Relativpronomen*

Eine Liebesgeschichte ...

1. **Verbinde beide Sätze. Ein Hauptsatz wird dabei zu einem Relativsatz!**

   Debbie is **the girl**. Tom is in love with **her**.

   _____

   Debbie is **the girl**. He is interested in **her**.

   _____

   Debbie is **the girl**. He dreams of **her**.

   _____

   Tom is **the boy**. Debbie is looking for **him**.

   _____

Welcher Film war es?

2. **Bilde Relativsätze. Lasse das Relativpronomen aus, wenn es nicht notwendig ist.**

   Do you know the film? It's on TV tonight.

   _____

   Do you know the actor? He plays the main character* in it.

   _____

   Didn't Richard Gere play a part in the film? You saw it some days ago.

   _____

   What was the title of the film? He was in the film.

   _____

   Didn't you see it with Debbie? You know the girl. She is Tom's friend.

   _____

   * main character = Hauptfigur

Test 102  Schwierigkeitsstufe

Die indirekte Rede – *Aussagesätze und Fragen in der indirekten Rede*

Ein Telefongespräch

1. Setze die folgenden Sätze in die indirekte Rede, nimm aber nicht immer das gleiche einleitende Verb. Möglich sind hier:

to say (to somebody)   to explain (to somebody)   to believe   to be sure   to think

to add   to shout   to answer   to know   to write

Debbie:

"I'm ill." _____.

"I have to stay in bed." _____.

"I've got the flu." _____.

"Mum called a doctor." _____.

Tom:

"I'm very sorry." _____.

"I hope you will feel better soon." _____.

"I'll tell Mr Mason that you're ill." _____.

Am nächsten Tag

2. Setze die folgenden Sätze in die indirekte Rede.

Tom asks / wants to know:

"Do you feel better today?" _____.

"Can you get up?" _____.

"Did the doctor come?" _____.

"Do you have to stay in bed?" _____.

"Can I come to see you?" _____.

"Have you taken any medicine?" _____.

Test 103 ▮▮☐ Schwierigkeitsstufe

Die indirekte Rede – *Aussagesätze und Fragen in der indirekten Rede*

Was du vielleicht noch weißt ...

1. Kreuze an, was richtig ist.

1. Um was für Satztypen handelt es sich in Aufgabe 2 in Test 102?

   ☐ a) Fragen ☐ b) Aussagesätze

2. Welche einleitenden Verben musst du gebrauchen?

   ☐ a) *to say* ☐ b) *to ask* ☐ c) *to want to know*

3. Welche Konjunktion musst du dann gebrauchen?

   ☐ a) *that* ☐ b) *if*

4. Wie sieht es mit der Wortstellung im Nebensatz aus? Musst du dieselbe Wortstellung

   ☐ a) wie in der Frage ☐ b) wie im Aussagesatz (SPO) gebrauchen?

5. Musst du im indirekten Fragesatz die *to do*-Umschreibung gebrauchen?

   ☐ a) ja ☐ b) nein

6. Muss am Satzende ein Fragezeichen stehen?

   ☐ a) ja ☐ b) nein

Auf ein Neues ...

2. Setze in die indirekte Rede.

Debbie's mother asks / wants to know *(in a conversation with the doctor)*:

"Can her friends visit her?" _____.

"Is she very ill?" _____.

"Has she got the flu?" _____.

"Does she feel very bad?" _____.

"Does she have a temperature?" _____.

"Will she get better soon?" _____.

Test 1

Aufgabe 1

books	plans
planes	minutes
answers	apples
faces	chairs
boxes	dresses
tables	pages
sandwiches	pencil cases
bridges	desks
hours	brushes
teachers	pupils

Aufgabe 2

pages	bridges
exercises	cornflakes
churches	messages
clothes	places
houses	brochures
faces	voices
roles	noises
stages	noses
theatres	horses
buses	scenes
titles	brushes
languages	cakes
phrases	classes
pieces	glasses
centres	tables

Test 2

Aufgabe 1

day	boy
baby	family
thief	play
wife	knife
shelf	country
party	life
half	hobby

Aufgabe 2

boys and girls	babies and toys
brothers and sisters	nights and days
books on shelves	diaries and pens
pupils and teachers	houses and flats
cats and dogs	buses and lorries
short lives	

Test 3

Aufgabe 1

children	countries
sheep	cakes
sandwiches	knives
men	

Aufgabe 2

foot	parents
food	family
breakfast	neighbours

Test 4

Aufgabe 1

Nur im Singular werden gebraucht: *news*, *mathematics*, *information*, *homework*. Als Plurale werden im Englischen immer *police* und *people* (= Leute, Menschen) gebraucht. Mit einem Plural-s bedeutet *peoples* im übrigen „Völker".

Aufgabe 2

a There is too much homework …
b … who think that homework is fun.
c These people are completely wrong …
d … there is some maths homework, and there is homework in …
e That is bad news again. But thanks for the information though it is not very good.

Test 5

Aufgabe 1

a man's world	children's playground
women's magazines	a child's toys
a woman's job	people's ideas
men's hobbies	girls' day

Aufgabe 2

They are grandpa's teeth, … my sister's baby, …Tom's parents, … that girl's jeans, … Mr Owen's children, … that boy's mum, … my parrot's cage, … twins' doll, … the cat's food

Test 6

Aufgabe 1

the legs of the table	the walls of the room
the book of the month	the roof of this house
the colour of your eyes	the girl of my dreams
the pages of this book	the plural of this word
the apple of my eye	the end of this exercise.
the photos of my sister	

Aufgabe 2

a Tom**'s** got a new friend. He**'s** the new boy in Tom<u>'s</u> class. Ken<u>'s</u> family is new here, too. Ken**'s** very good at maths. He can be very helpful, so most pupils in Tom<u>'s</u> class like him. Ken**'s** got a pet, too. It**'s** a hamster. He must look after it, clean its cage and buy the hamster<u>'s</u> food.

b Tom has got … He is the new boy … Ken is very good … Ken has got … It is a hamster.

LÖSUNGEN

Test 7

Aufgabe 1
an easy question   an expensive pullover
an interesting lesson   a beautiful voice
a terrible/silly/boy   a new book
an unhappy/a sad teacher a nice boy

Aufgabe 2
a, a, an, an, a, an. Das nächste Wort beginnt mit einem Konsonant, Konsonant , Vokal, Vokal, einem sogenannten Halbvokal /ju/, Vokal.

Test 8

Aufgabe 1
a Mit/ði/werden ausgesprochen: the English lesson, the easy tests, the exciting exercises, the unhappy pupils, the interesting subjects, the old churches. Vor Vokal wird the wie/ði /, vor Konsonant und Halbvokal wie/ðə/ausgesprochen.
b Es gelten dieselben Regeln wie für den Gebrauch von *a/an*.

Aufgabe 2
He has got a temperature. He has got a sore throat. He has got a headache, too. Has he got a cold? Well, I think he has got a bad cold or he has got the flu. It's a pity he can't come to our party.

Test 9

Aufgabe 1
This is my schoolbag and that is your schoolbag.
This is my seat and that is your seat.
This is my sandwich and that is your sandwich.
These are my books and those are your books.
These are my pencils and those are your pencils.
These are my CDs and those are your CDs.
This is my iPod and that is your iPod.
These are my things and those are your things.
This is my mobile and that is her mobile.
And this is my girlfriend; don't think she is yours!

Aufgabe 2
Look at this pullover. It's really nice and that pullover is very nice, too. Which pullover is nicer, this pullover or that pullover over there? Look! Aren't they lovely? Those t-shirts right in front of you? And what about these t-shirts right here? I like these t-shirts here better. Can we go in and buy one? Okay, but let's have a look at those shirts in the shop window, too.

Test 10

Aufgabe 1
our friends   their rooms
your bikes   their bones
their cars

Aufgabe 2
Ihre   Ihr
dein   dein
eure

Test 11

Aufgabe 1
... It's a big school. It's a new school, too ... He thinks it's a good school and that it's fun to go there.

Aufgabe 2
Look, that Tom's house over there.
Where? There, on your left.
That's their house? ...
There is a big garden behind it.
We often play there.
Oh, can we go there, too?

Test 12

Aufgabe 1
Mögliche Antworten:
He/she is nice and young, but not very funny.
He/she is young and clever, but not very exciting.
She is good-looking and funny, but sometimes a bit loud.
He is loud and strong, but very intelligent etc.

Aufgabe 2
Mögliche Antworten:
Football is wonderful and exciting.
Computers are useful and fast.
Boys are loud and stupid.
Shopping is boring and expensive.
Comics are cheap and funny.
Pop stars are crazy and often very loud.
Girls are nice and good-looking.
Casting shows are stupid and boring.
English lessons are great, fantastic, exciting, wonderful!

Test 13

Aufgabe 1
rich, richer, the richest
cheap, cheaper, the cheapest
long, longer, the longest
loud, louder, the loudest

Aufgabe 2
nice, nicer, the nicest   thin, thinner, the thinnest
large, larger, the largest   hot, hotter, the hottest
big, bigger, the biggest   fat, fatter, the fattest

Test 14

Aufgabe 1
good, better, the best
bad, worse, the worst
much/many, more, the most

Aufgabe 2
Most pupils think …
This is a mistake most pupils make.
Most mistakes … the most idiotic.
Sheila is the most beautiful girl … Most pupils …
Ben thinks that most girls …
He only forgets that he is the most stupid boy in our class.

Aufgabe 3
dangerous, more dangerous, the most dangerous
dirty, dirtier, the dirtiest
interesting, more interesting, the most interesting
careful, more careful, the most careful
quick, quicker, the quickest

Test 15

Aufgabe 1
1 cold, colder, the coldest
   funny, funnier, the funniest
   simple, simpler, the simplest
2 nice, nicer, the nicest
   easy, easier, the easiest
3 expensive, more expensive, the most expensive
   beautiful, more beautiful, the most beautiful
4 good, better, the best
   bad, worse, the worst

Test 16

Aufgabe 1
Mögliche Antworten:
Football is (not) as interesting as tennis.
Swimming is (not) as boring as running.
English is (not) as difficult as German.
Morning lessons are (not) as bad as afternoon lessons.
Books are (not) as interesting as comics.
I am (not) as intelligent as my neighbour.
Dolls are (not) as interesting as toy cars.

Aufgabe 2
Mögliche Antworten:
Football is more interesting than tennis.
Swimming is more boring than running.
German is more difficult than English.
Afternoon lessons are worse than morning lessons.
Books are more interesting than comics.
I am more intelligent than my neighbour.
Dolls are more interesting than toy cars.

Test 17

Aufgabe 1
What were you doing then? I was reading a book then. More interesting than the other one? Aren't women as intelligent as men? … men are better than women… they are as good as women … worse than women. Fine, then you seem to know …

Aufgabe 2
2 This mistake is bad. That mistake is worse, but those mistakes are the worst.
3 Sue is a smart girl, but Alice is smarter. Debbie is the smartest girl of the three.
4 This test is difficult, but the English test is more difficult. The maths test is the most difficult.
5 Bob is noisy, but his neighbour is noisier. John is the noisiest of all.

Test 18

Aufgabe 1
Does anybody/anyone know him?
Has anybody/anyone seen him?
Did he go anywhere?
Can you see him anywhere?
Did he do anything? No, he didn't do anything.
Did he talk to anybody/anyone?

Aufgabe 2
Somebody/Someone must talk to him.
We must do something about him.
But what can we do? Can we really do anything?
We must find some help somewhere.
We must find somebody to help him.
If we don't, something terrible will happen.

Test 19

Aufgabe 1
Some in bejahten Sätzen, *any* in Fragen; *not … any* in verneinten Sätzen.

Aufgabe 2
a Hier wird eine positive Antwort erwartet.
b Can I have some money, please? … Didn't I give you some money yesterday? I really think I did. I hope you have got some left. Let's clean the car. Can somebody/someone come and help me? I really need some help. Well, here's your chance. I'll give you some extra money if you help me.

LÖSUNGEN

Test 20

Aufgabe 1
... He works from morning to night. He works in the morning, in the afternoon, in the evening, even on Saturdays and on Sundays. He seldom goes to bed before midnight. He gets up very early, at about 6. After a short breakfast he settles down to work. Nothing can stop him. Last year he even worked on his birthday and even on December, 25th, Christmas Day. Let's wish him a Merry Christmas this year!

Aufgabe 2
Tom was born in 1997.
His birthday is in April.
It's on April 2nd.
His friend's birthday is on the same day.
It's on a Friday this year.
On Saturday they are going to have a big party.
It's always fun to have parties at the weekend!
    (AmE = on the weekend), It will begin at 3 o'clock
    and end at 11.
They'll prepare for the party from morning to night on
    Friday.

Test 21

Aufgabe 1
It's on the right/on the left/in the middle.
They are on/under/in the wardrobe.
They are on the wall.
It's in the middle, on the left, on the right, in front of ...
What is on your desk?
What's behind your bed?

Aufgabe 2
... Tom's still in his room ... His English textbook is still on his desk. ... books are lying on the floor near/under his bed. His pencil-case is also on the desk in front of/near his computer. ...everything into/in his schoolbag. The bus is already waiting at the bus stop. Tom runs to the bus stop, but he doesn't make it. So he has to go to school by bike. ... he rushes into the classroom ... He's standing in front of/near/at the board with the register in his hands ... You couldn't get out of bed this morning, could you?

Test 22

Aufgabe 1
They are not at home. They are not in their room. Near the house there is a field. Are they playing in the field? It's not very far from the house. Or are they in the street? There is a garden round (AmE = around) the house ... They are in the living-room in front of the telly ...Oh, look, here it is, on page 12 of the TV guide.

Aufgabe 2
1 b), 2 e), 3 f), 4 a), 5 d), 6 h), 7 g), 8 c)

Test 23

Aufgabe 1
I am Tom.
Are you new here?
Where are you from?
... Are they from Bristol, too?
... Is it new?
Have you got a sister?
How old is she?
Is she in your class?
Is she nice?
Can I meet her?

Aufgabe 2
It is not here. I can't find it. It must still be ...
... Is it ...?
... I think it is on the bus.
What are you doing ...? Are you doing ...?
No, sir, we are ...
What! You are ...
Yes, sir, we are.

Test 24

Aufgabe 1

me	us
you	you
him	them
her	them
it	them

Aufgabe 2
a du, ihr, Sie, Sie
b dir, dich, euch, Sie, Ihnen, Sie, Ihnen

Test 25

Aufgabe 1

mich/mir	es/ihm
ihn/ihm	uns/uns
sie/ihr	sie/ihnen

Aufgabe 2

I can't see/find it	them
it	it
them	them
it	it
her	they
him	

Test 26

Aufgabe 1
a im Wem-Fall (= Dativ)
b im Wen-Fall (= Akkusativ)
c nach einer Präposition

LÖSUNGEN

Aufgabe 2
... Everybody is looking for them, but nobody can find them. Where are they hiding? The children are looking for Alice first. Where is she? Is she in Tom's room? No, she isn't in the room. It is empty. There is no trace of her there. Is she under Tom's bed? No, she isn't. Is she behind the door? No, she isn't. She isn't behind it. Where is she then? She is in the wardrobe, with Ken! They are hiding behind some clothes, so nobody can find them. But they are laughing, so the children can hear them.

Test 27

Aufgabe 1

mine	ours
yours	yours
hers	theirs
his	

Aufgabe 2
... This table is ours.
... Yours is over there.
... Ben. It isn't yours.
Those aren't your seats, Ken und Sam. Yours are over there.
Is this your glass? No, ... It's hers.
... Debbie? Yes, It's mine. ...
... Yes, it is. It's his.
...They are theirs.
... I don't think it's mine. ...
Yes, it's hers.

Test 28

Aufgabe 1
Which ones?
The green one and the blue one ...
... Look at the red one ...
... that one over there?
... the yellow one.
Yes, that one. The one with Beg Ben on it.
... that yellow one.

Aufgabe 2
Excuse me, could I try on that yellow pullover?
Which one?
The one over there with Ben Big on it.
... a bigger one?
... the only one left.
... show me the red one over there?
... Oh, I like this one very much.

Test 29

Aufgabe 1

badly	beautifully
quickly	completely
nervously	noisily
stupidly	terribly
carefully	horribly
nicely	hard
slowly	lazily
quietly	simply
dangerously	fast
excitedly	well

Aufgabe 2
a awfully, cruelly, gratefully, officially, really, usefully
b largely, nicely, safely, politely, strangely, aggressively
c busily, crazily, luckily, happily, noisily

Test 30

Aufgabe 1

I sing beautifully.	I work hard.
I drive carefully.	I always answer
I play tennis well.	questions intelligently.
I swim fast.	I dance excellently.

Aufgabe 2
1 Ken likes Alice very much. Ben likes her more, but John likes her most.
2 Tom sings well. Bob sings better, but Robert sings best.
3 Mike speaks German badly. John speaks it worse, but Kevin speaks it worst.
4 Sue works hard. Alice works harder, but Kate works hardest.

Test 31

Aufgabe 1
a (1) as well as (2) better than (3) better than (4) as fast as (5) faster than (6) as elegantly as (7) harder than
b Bei (not) as ... as ... steht die Grundform des Adverbs. Bei *than* steht immer der Komparativ.

Aufgabe 2
a faster than
b much more carefully than
c as cleverly as
d worse than
e much more calmly than
f as easily as Tom

LÖSUNGEN

Test 32

Aufgabe 1

a A man <u>and</u> his dog are walking along a road. Suddenly the man remembers <u>that</u> he <u>and</u> his dog are already dead. He stops for a moment, <u>but</u> then he walks on. After some time they come to a high, white wall. <u>When</u> they get near it, they see a big door in the wall <u>and</u> realize <u>that</u> the street which leads into it is made of pure gold. Then they see a man who is standing there. <u>When</u> they get near enough, they ask him where they are. The man tells them <u>that</u> this place is called heaven.

b Sie verbinden gleiche Satzteile (z. B. zwei Substantive) oder einen Haupt- mit einem Nebensatz.

Aufgabe 2

a *and* = und; *or* = oder; *but* = aber; *so* = so; *if* = wenn, falls/ob; *when* = wenn; *that* = dass; *so that* = sodass; *because* = weil; *although* = obwohl; *before* = bevor; *until* = bis

b Konjunktionen wie *and, or, but, so* verbinden gleiche Satzteile (z. B. zwei Substantive) oder gleiche Satzarten (z. B. zwei Hauptsätze), Konjunktionen wie *if, when* dagegen verbinden Hauptsätze mit Nebensätzen.

Test 33

Aufgabe 1

... Many/a lot of people are there, including many/a lot of pupils in Tom's class. There are many/a lot of stalls there, too ... You can see a many/lot of photos at their stall. ... they play a lot of music and have a lot of fun. They also have a chess club, where you can meet many/a lot of chess players ... There are many/a lot of bikes at their stall. ... so many/a lot pupils visit their stall.

Aufgabe 2

a How much is this bike? It costs too much money!
How many bikes have you got here?
How many bikes can you repair ...?
How much money does it cost ...?
How many girls ...?
How much time ...? I spend so much time there!
How many pupils ...?

b Nach dem Fragewort *how*, und nach den Adverbien *so* und *too*, ist nur *much* oder *many* möglich.

Test 34

Aufgabe 1

Mike hasn't got any friends/any money/any parents/any brothers and sisters/any family/any food at home/any fun.

Aufgabe 2

Is there any good film on tonight?
... I haven't got any money on me.
I hope you have got some.
... I haven't got any money on me either.
... Have you got any ideas?
... Perhaps she has got some money and can lend us some ...
But Alice has got no time and no money. ... Poor Tom and Ken! They're not having any luck tonight!

Test 35

Aufgabe 1

... but many/a lot of/some/a few of his sentences are not correct. He makes many/a lot of/some/a few mistakes. You need a little/a lot of/some time to understand him. ... He only likes a few/some things. Some/Many vegetables are a real horror to him and he doesn't eat any/a lot of meat. He also doesn't drink any/much milk. What he likes, are sweets, but too many sweets aren't good for him.

Aufgabe 2

deutsche Bedeutung	Substantiv im Singular	Substantiv im Plural
viel(e)	much/a lot of	many/a lot of
wenig(e)	little	few
ein paar/einige	–	a few/some
ein bisschen	little	–
etwas	some	–
kein(e)	no/not ... any	no/not ... any

Test 36

Aufgabe 1

Mögliche Lösungen:

a cup of coffee   a bar of chocolate
a glass of milk   a tin of peas
a bowl of soup   a box of oranges
a plate of sausages   a bottle of lemonade
a piece of cake   a pound of butter
a bag of crisps   a pair of shoes
a slice of bread   a list of names

Aufgabe 2

a glass/cup/bottle of water   a cup/pot of tea
a box/pound of apples   a bottle/glass of milk
a bowl/a bag of crisps   a bar/piece of chocolate

Test 37

Aufgabe 1

How many boys/girls/desks etc. are there in your school/class/classroom?
There are _____ boys/girls/desks etc. in my school/in my class/in my classroom.

Aufgabe 2
There are 15 pairs of trainers, two right shoes, seven left shoes, four shirts, six anoraks, eight socks and five English textbooks in the caretaker's room. There is also one schoolbag.

Test 38

Aufgabe 1

a 29 – twenty-nine
b 37 – thirty-seven
c 75 – seventy-five
d 71 – seventy-one
e 58 – fifty-eight
f 25 – twenty-five

Aufgabe 2
three, thirteen, thirty-three
four, fourteen, forty-four
five, fifteen, fifty-five
eight, eighteen, eighty-eight
nine, nineteen, ninety-nine

Test 39

Aufgabe 1
It's six o'clock
half past six (AmE = six thirty)
a quarter to seven (AmE = six forty-five)
a quarter past seven (AmE = seven fifteen)
ten to nine (AmE = eight fifty)
twenty-five to ten, thirty-five past nine (AmE = nine thirty-five)
twenty past ten (AmE = ten twenty)
half past ten (AmE = ten thirty)
twenty to twelve (AmE = eleven forty)
five to twelve (AmE = eleven fifty-five)

Aufgabe 2
Tom's first lesson is from ten to nine to twenty to ten.
PE is from a quarter to ten to twenty-five to eleven.
Break is from twenty-five to eleven to ten to eleven.
Maths is from five to eleven to a quarter to twelve.
Geography is from ten to twelve to twenty to one.
Lunch is from twenty to one to twenty to two.
Music is from a quarter to two to half past two.

Test 40

Aufgabe 1
a/one hundred
two hundred
three hundred and forty-five
eight hundred and eighty-eight
a/one thousand
two thousand
one hundred thousand
one million

Aufgabe 2
seventeen hundred and seventy-six
two thousand eight
eighteen hundred and eight-eight
ten hundred and sixty-six
sixteen hundred and sixty-eight
ten hundred and ninety-six
two thousand forty-nine

Test 41

Aufgabe 1

the first
the second
the third
the fourth
the fifth
the eighth
the ninth
the eleventh

the twelfth
the fourteenth
the fifteenth
the nineteenth
the twentieth
the thirty-first
the forty-fourth
the sixty-seventh

Aufgabe 2

February
the twelfth month
twenty-fifth
May
August

the second day
Friday
Monday
the sixth lesson
the third lesson

Test 42

Aufgabe 1

Wednesday
February
October
Thursday
Monday

January
August
Saturday
March
Tuesday

Aufgabe 2

It's on a Friday.
It's on a Wednesday.
It's on a Tuesday.
It's on a Saturday.

It's on a Thursday.
It's on a Sunday.
It's on a _____.

Test 43

Aufgabe 1
the seventeenth of December, nineteen fifty-six
the twenty-eighth of June, nineteen forty
the twenty-fifth of July, two thousand eight
the nineteenth of April, nineteen thirteen
the third of December, two thousand one

Aufgabe 2
New Year's Day is on the first of January.
Boxing Day is on the twenty-sixth of December.
Christmas Day is on the twenty-fifth of December.
May Day is on the first of May.
Summer Bank Holiday is on the twenty-seventh of August.

LÖSUNGEN

Test 44

Aufgabe 1
Excuse me, are you Tom?
Are you from Bristol?
Is that your sister?
Is she in your class?
What is her name?
How old is she?
Are these boys in your class, too?
Is that your classroom?
Is the man over there a teacher?

Aufgabe 2
a No, I'm not.
b No, they aren't.
c Yes, they are.
d Yes, we are.
e Yes, I am.
f Yes, I am.
g No, they aren't.
h No, it isn't.
i Yes, of course they are!

Test 45

Aufgabe 1
Mögliche Antworten:
Yes, there are./No, there aren't.
Yes, there are./No, there aren't.
Yes, there are./No, there aren't.
Yes, there is./No, there isn't.
Yes, there is./No, there isn't.
Yes, there is./No, there isn't.
Yes, there are./No, there aren't.
Yes, there is./No, there isn't.

Aufgabe 2
Yes, it is.
No, it isn't.
Yes, it is.
Yes, it is.
No, it isn't.
Yes, it is.
No, it isn't.
Yes, it is.

Test 46

Aufgabe 1
Who are you?
How are you?
What is his name?
Who is your friend?
How old are you?
Where are the other boys?
Where is your bike?
Where is your sister?
Who is your English teacher?
What is that on your chair?
What kind of book is it?

Aufgabe 2
Where are you?
What's your name?
Where are you from?
What's your father's name?
How old are you?
Where are your parents?
Who is your friend?

Test 47

Aufgabe 1
Sam hasn't got a brother, but he's got an aunt.
Ken hasn't got a sister, but he's got a brother.
The Bensons haven't got a flat. They've got a house.
Emma has got a bike. She hasn't got a car.
Alice has got a mobile phone, but she hasn't got a computer.

Aufgabe 2
a Have you got a sister, Sam? No, I haven't got a sister, but I've got an aunt.
b Have you got a sister, Ken? No, I haven't got a sister, but I've got a brother.
c Have you got a flat, Mr and Mrs Benson? No, we haven't got a flat. We've got a house.
d Has Emma got a bike? Yes, she has got a bike, but she hasn't got a car.

Test 48

Aufgabe 1
Mögliche Antworten:
Yes, it is./No, it isn't.
Yes, there are./No, there aren't.
Yes, I have./No, I haven't.
Yes, I have./No, I haven't.
Yes, they are./No, they aren't.
Yes, they have./No, they haven't.
Yes, I have./No, I haven't.
Yes, I am./No, I'm not.
Yes, they are./No, they aren't.
Yes, I am./No, I'm not.
Yes, it is./No, it isn't.

Aufgabe 2
haven't
have
isn't
aren't
have
has
are
have

Test 49

Aufgabe 1
a I can speak English, but I can't speak Spanish.
Can we see each other tomorrow, Alice? No, I can't. I'm busy.
May I smoke here, sir? No, you may not.
May I do my homework here? Yes, you may.
b *can* bedeutet, dass man etwas tun kann oder auch (umgangsprachlich) tun darf. *May* bedeutet ebenfalls „dürfen", ist aber förmlicher als *can*.

Aufgabe 2
May I ask you a question, sir?
Yes, you may.
May I leave the classroom, sir? ...
... I must go to the toilet, sir. May I leave the classroom now?
John, just have a look at your watch. Can you tell me the time?
Yes, I can. It's three minutes to twelve.
Well, John, then you certainly can wait another three minutes.
Oh sir, I hope I can.

Test 50

Aufgabe 1

What can I do for you?	What must you do?
How can I help you?	Where must you go?
Why can't you help me?	

Aufgabe 2
I must always do what others tell me.
I must get up early.
I mustn't miss the bus.
I must do my homework.
I must stay at school all day long.

Test 51

Aufgabe 1

I must stay in bed.	I needn't go to school.
I must take my medicine.	I mustn't play football.
I needn't do my homework.	I must see a doctor.

Aufgabe 2
Mögliche Antworten:
I needn't clean the classroom.
I needn't/mustn't kiss my teacher.
I mustn't talk to my neighbour.
I mustn't smoke at school.
I mustn't call my teacher names.
I must listen to my teacher.
I must do my homework.
I mustn't fight with my neighbour.

Test 52

Aufgabe 1

Komm ...	Kommen Sie ...
Kommt ...	Kommen Sie ...
Kommen Sie ...	

Aufgabe 2

Come back soon.	Brush your teeth.
Be here at seven.	Do your homework.
Pull/Pick up your socks.	Help me now.
Eat up your soup.	Set the table.
Tidy up your room.	Do the dishes.
Have a bath or a shower.	Go to bed now.
Wash your hands.	

Test 53

Aufgabe 1

cleaning	fixing
laughing	playing
drinking	trying
shouting	singing
watching	fighting
buying	listening
crying	doing
washing	going
talking	saying
eating	carrying
knocking	

Aufgabe 2

writing	clapping
coming	stopping
changing	getting
tripping	dying
sitting	losing
dropping	taking
cutting	driving
lying	putting
choosing	running
riding	swimming
having	forgetting
planning	tying

Test 54

Aufgabe 1
They are eating their sandwiches.
They are standing together in groups.
They are talking.
Somebody is shouting.
Some children are playing.
Two pupils are fighting.
Somebody is calling a teacher.

Aufgabe 2
The pupils are leaving the schoolyard.
They are going into the school building.
Some are running.
A pupil is lying on the floor.
He is crying.
A teacher is coming.
The teacher is carrying him into the office.
He is putting him on a stretcher.
The secretary is getting him a glass of water.
She is calling an ambulance.

LÖSUNGEN

Test 55

Aufgabe 1
Is Tom sitting in his chair?
Is he doing an exercise?
Are Kevin and Ken making the girls angry?
Is Alice flirting with Mike?
Is Robert lying on the floor?
Are Bob, Ben and John playing cards?
Is Debbie reading a magazine?
Is Fiona running around the classroom?
Is Tim playing football in the classroom?

Aufgabe 2
Yes, she is.
No, he isn't.
No, they aren't.
No, she isn't.
No, they aren't.

Yes, he is.
No, he isn't.
No, she isn't.
No, they aren't.
No, he isn't.

Test 56

Aufgabe 1
What are you looking for?
Who are you waiting for?
Who are you looking at?
What are you listening to?
What are you talking about?
Who are you looking after?
Who are you thinking of? *(think of = denken an think about = nachdenken über)*
Why are you running away?
What are you writing down?
What word are you looking up?
What are you putting in your bag?
What trousers are you trying on?

Aufgabe 2
to get off a bus
to turn it off
to take it off

to put them on
to wake up
to sit down

Test 57

Aufgabe 1
When the Bensons come home ...
Then they have tea.
After tea they wash up the dishes.
Tom sometimes helps them.
Then Mr Benson reads his newspaper.
Mrs Benson reads ...
Later they watch TV.
Mr Benson likes films. His wife does so, too.
At about eleven they go to bed.

Aufgabe 2
... don't get up early.
... doesn't go to work.
... don't have an early breakfast.
... don't make their beds.
... doesn't do any homework.

... doesn't go to school.
... doesn't do the gardening.
... don't stay at home all day.

Test 58

Aufgabe 1
Subjekt: *who/what*; Verb: *what*; Objekt: *who/what*;
Ort: *where*; Zeit: *when*

Aufgabe 2
a Who sees Tom ...? What shows its top cars ...?
b What does Debbie do ...? What does the shop do ...?
c Who does Debbie see ...? What does the shop show ...?
d Where does Debbie see Tom at 9? Where does the shop show its top cars this week?
e When does Debbie see Tom in the classroom? When does the shop show its top cars?

Test 59

Aufgabe 1
a what für Sachen, who für Personen
b what
c nicht bei positiven Fragen nach dem Subjekt
d im Singular

Aufgabe 2
Who works as a caretaker at Tom's school?
Where does Mr Hedges work?
Who likes his job?
What does he like?
Who likes him?
Who do children like?

Test 60

Aufgabe 1
how
how
why
how

which
why
what

Aufgabe 2
Do you like (watching) TV?
What do you normally watch on TV?
What kind of films do you like?
What do your parents say about them/the films?
What other programmes do you watch?
How often do you turn on the TV?
How long do you watch TV?
When do you turn off the TV?
Do you sometimes fall asleep in front of the TV?
When do you go to bed?

Test 61

Aufgabe 1
The Bensons get up at seven. They wash and dress.
Then they have breakfast. At 8 they leave the house.
Mrs Benson takes the bus. She works in a hospital.
She looks after patients. She has lunch there, too.
Mr Benson works for a newspaper. He writes and
corrects articles. He often has lunch in town. The
Bensons come home in the early evening. Then they
have tea or supper.

Aufgabe 2

oft	nie/niemals
immer	manchmal
oft	immer
gewöhnlich/normaler-	selten
weise	nie
manchmal	

Test 62

Aufgabe 1
1 No, I don't. I never drive my teachers crazy.
2 Yes, I am. I am seldom unfriendly.
3 Yes, I am. I'm always happy when I go to school.
4 Yes, they do. They usually give me good marks.
5 Yes, I do. I always listen to them.

Aufgabe 2
Mögliche Antworten:
Every morning I brush my teeth.
Every afternoon I play computer games with friends.
Every day I get older.
Every week I get pocket money from my parents.
Every year I get a birthday present.

Test 63

Aufgabe 1
a The sun is shining.
  It's not raining.
  The birds are singing.
  And we are sitting indoors!
  We are doing a test.
  Look! Mike is dreaming.
  He is listening to the birds.
  Our teacher is trying to talk to Mike.
b Die Handlung läuft gerade ab, ist also noch nicht
  abgeschlossen.

Aufgabe 2
next year, *then*, *the next day*, *every morning*, *after that*, *the
next evening*, *seldom* sind **keine** Signalwörter für das
present progressive.

Test 64

Aufgabe 1

know	want
understand	love
be	hear
like	see

Aufgabe 2
Alice often watches TV, but this evening she doesn't
  want to watch anything.
She wants to go out. Today is her girlfriend's birthday,
  and there will be a party at her house.
Alice wants to be there, but her mother doesn't like her
  friends.
She doesn't understand why Alice has such friends.
What can Alice do? Look! She is in her room.
She is standing in front of the mirror. She is putting on
her new dress and a bit of make-up!
What is she doing?! She is going out.
Does she always do things like that?
Yes, she always does what she wants!

Test 65

Aufgabe 1
a Were .../Yes, I was.
b Were .../No, I wasn't.   f Was .../No, she wasn't.
c Were .../Yes, they were.   g Was .../Yes, she was.
d Were .../Yes, they were.   h Was/No, she wasn't.
e Were .../No, they weren't. i Were/Yes, I was.

Aufgabe 2
Why were you not at school last week?
How long were you ill?
Why were you ill?
When were you better again?
How many of your friends were there?
Who was missing?
Why was Debbie not there?
Where was the doctor?

Test 66

Aufgabe 1
When the doorbell rang yesterday at seven o'clock ...
I was just getting up.
my parents were having breakfast.
my father was reading the morning paper.
my sister was still sleeping.
our neighbors were still lying in their beds.
my younger brother was still dreaming.
other people were having a good time.

LÖSUNGEN

Aufgabe 2
Yesterday at 11 am …
most people were not lying in their beds anymore.
my parents were not having breakfast anymore.
most people were not sleeping anymore.
I was not lying in my bed anymore either.
I was not sitting at the breakfast table anymore.
I was not playing football.
I was sitting on a chair.
I was doing an English test.

Test 67

Aufgabe 1
a happened, knocked, passed, pushed;
turned, watched, cheered, cooked, talked;
answered, asked, climbed, finished;
explained, guessed, helped, looked;
stayed, played, enjoyed
b loved, danced, explored, agreed
c invited, hated, pointed, ended, folded
d hurried, cried, carried, tidied
e planned, dropped, stopped, clapped

Aufgabe 2
1 … wird ein -ed angehängt.
2 … wie /id/ ausgesprochen.
3 … nach Konsonant zu ie, nach Vokal bleibt es erhalten.
4 … wird verdoppelt.

Test 68

Aufgabe 1

chose	read
came	went
did	gave
drove	hid
kept	rode
lost	spoke
met	stood
had	took
heard	told
hurt	threw
sold	knew
ate	wrote
flew	wore
fell	fought
felt	meant
left	found
made	

Aufgabe 2
1 cut, <u>got</u>, put, cost
2 knew, flew, grew, <u>showed</u>
3 drank, sang, began, <u>won</u>
4 slept, kept, felt, <u>saw</u>
5 <u>caught</u>, thought, brought, bought

Test 69

Aufgabe 1

they didn't find …	The burglar was not …
There weren't …	He didn't make …
They didn't see …	He didn't want …
There weren't …	The police were not…

Aufgabe 2
a *did not* oder *didn't*
b Infinitiv
c von *to do*. Hier genügt ein *not*.
d

they didn't see	they didn't notice
they didn't find	they didn't hear
they didn't listen	this didn't mean
I didn't understand	they were not
I didn't do	we didn't do

Test 70

Aufgabe 1
a Did you call us …?
b Did you leave the window open?
c Did anybody know …?
d Did you turn the lights on?
e Did you notice anything …?
f Did your neighbour notice anything?
g Were you out all evening?
h Did you shut that door?
i Did the burglar steal anything?
j Did he open that safe?

Aufgabe 2

a Yes, we did.	f No, he/she didn't.
b No, we didn't.	g Yes, we were.
c No, nobody did.	h No, we didn't.
d Yes, we did.	i Yes, he did.
e Yes, we did.	j Yes, he did.

Test 71

Aufgabe 1
1 who/what
2 Bei nicht verneinten Fragen nach dem Subjekt.
3 Bei Fragen nach allen anderen Satzteilen muss man *to do* gebrauchen.

Aufgabe 2
Who broke into the house?
Who didn't the neighbours see?
What did he open?
Who took the money out of the safe?
What did he take out of the safe?

Test 72

Aufgabe 1
... the sun was shining.
... the sun was not hiding behind clouds.
... many people were there.
... many people were swimming in the pool.
... others were talking to their friends.
... others were playing football.
... some people were sleeping.
... some were reading a book or a magazine.
... some were lying in the sun and dreaming.

Aufgabe 2
People were not shouting.
People were not running around.
People were not fighting.
Mike was lying peacefully in the grass.
Ken was not screaming at the others.
Only John was telling silly stories.

Test 73

Aufgabe 1
Yesterday we went to the zoo .... We walked to the bus stop. We got on the bus. In the bus we looked for our seats. Everybody was happy. But soon the trouble started. Mike didn't feel very well. He got sick. It was terrible!

Aufgabe 2
Some pupils started to run around in the bus.
Others began to eat their crisps.
There were crisps everywhere.
Other pupils put their feet on the seats.
The bus driver saw this.
He became angry.
He began to shout.
The bus arrived at the zoo.
We got off the bus.
I was happy.
We were there.

Test 74

Aufgabe 1
Suddenly the bus came to a stop. John was still standing when it stopped, and he fell onto the floor and hit his head on a seat. One of the pupils called Mr Winterbottom at once. He became very angry when he saw that John was lying on the floor. "Why don't you listen?" he shouted. But when he saw that John's mouth was bleeding, he ran to the bus driver and asked him to call a doctor. A few minutes later an ambulance arrived. Two paramedics came into the bus. They had a look at the boy. Then they fetched a stretcher. They put John on it and loaded him onto the ambulance.

Aufgabe 2
I was having a shower when I slipped. I crashed onto the floor. I was cleaning the windows when one window broke, and the broken glass cut my hands. John: I was running around on the bus when it suddenly stopped. I fell and hit my head on a seat.

Test 75

Aufgabe 1
<u>must</u>, <u>can't</u>, <u>can</u>, <u>can't</u>, <u>must</u>, <u>mustn't</u>, <u>needn't;</u> The paramedics took John to the accident and emergency department. He had to wait for a doctor. He felt better, but he couldn't move. So he could only stay where he was. He couldn't walk around the room. When the nurse came in, she told him that he had to stay where he was and that he was not allowed to stand up. But she also told him that he didn't have to worry.

Aufgabe 2
konnte = could
konnte nicht = couldn't
durfte = was/were allowed to
durfte nicht = was/were not allowed to
mustn't = was not/were not allowed to
musste nicht, brauchte nicht = didn't have to/didn't need to

Test 76

Aufgabe 1
John was allowed to go home.
He didn't have to stay in hospital.
He didn't have to go to school.
He had to stay in bed for three days.
His friends could come to see him, ...
... but they were not allowed to stay more than half an hour.
After 30 minutes they had to leave.

Aufgabe 2
Were you allowed to go home?
Didn't you have to stay in hospital?
Didn't you have to go to school?
Did you have to stay in bed?
Were you allowed to watch TV?
Were your friends allowed to visit you?
Were they allowed to stay with you?
Could they talk with you?
When did they have to leave?

Test 77

Aufgabe 1
Shall I carry it for you?
Shall I find a place for you to sleep?
Shall I buy a sandwich for you?
Shall I do it for you?
Shall I explain it to you?
Shall I keep you company?

Aufgabe 2
a   You shouldn't stay up so late.
b   You should study harder.
c   You shouldn't watch so much TV.
d   You should buy new ones.
e   You shouldn't eat so much.
f   You should wash it.
g   You should tidy it up.
h   You should look for them.
i   You should ask her out on a date..
j   You should go home now.

Test 78

Aufgabe 1
a   *Could* bedeutet hier „ könnte(st)". *Could* kann auch
noch „konnte" bedeuten.
b   Mit *could* (könnte) kannst du hölflich fragen oder ein
Angebot oder eine Möglichkeit ausdrücken.

Aufgabe 2
Would you like some more sugar?
Could you give me a piece of cake?
Do you want some more milk?
I don't want to go home.

Test 79

Aufgabe 1
Mr Fletcher doesn't have anything.
He doesn't have a house.
He doesn't have a wife.
He doesn't have a family.
He doesn't have a job.
He doesn't have any money.
He doesn't have a car.
He doesn't have any friends.
He doesn't have anything.

Aufgabe 2
Do your parents have a house?
Does Debbie have a hamster?
Do her parents have a cat?
Do you have a problem?
Does Mike have a bike?
Do these people have the tickets?
Does this girl have a friend?
Do you have a lot of courage?

Test 80

Aufgabe 1
They always have an argument ... First she has a shower
... After that she has a chat with her dolls. ... Alice
has/has got many of them. So when Alice goes to the
bathroom first, the others have/have got little time to
use it. They can't have a shower or a bath. ... they have
time to have a very quick breakfast ...

Aufgabe 2
... No, you can't, I am having a shower. Come on, Alice,
hurry up! We want to have a shower, too. Just go and
have your breakfast. You can have a shower after that ...
She is having a chat with her dolls now. They have the
day off, so they have/have got a lot of time. So there is
no need to have an argument today!

Test 81

Aufgabe 1
They had to (pay the bills/clean the flat/go to
work/listen to me) though they didn't want to.

Aufgabe 2
a   1 b, 2 a, I had to see you.   b   1   must
                                         2   must
                                         3   have to
                                         4   have to

Test 82

Aufgabe 1

talked	danced
ended	played
tried	returned
carried	killed
dropped	stopped
looked	died
tied	painted

Sie werden genauso gebildet wie die regelmäßigen
Formen des *simple past*.

Aufgabe 2

been	had
chosen	lost
flown	known
felt	fallen
written	thought
gone	done
said	told
worn	bought

Test 83

Aufgabe 1
Tom has been to school.
He has just come back.
His mum has been shopping.
She has bought a lot of things.
She has done the cooking.
She has cleaned the bathroom.
Tom has helped her.
They have had a busy day.
They have done a lot of things.

Aufgabe 2

a Tom's father has been very busy, too.
He has left the house.
But he has not been in his office.
He has not helped his wife.
He has been away on business.
He has taken the train to London.

b Sie stehen immer hinter dem Partizip.

Test 84

Aufgabe 1

No, we haven't.   No, we haven't.
No, we haven't.   Yes, we have.
No, we haven't.   No, we haven't.

Aufgabe 2

a ever = jemals; yet = schon; not yet = noch nicht;
already = schon, bereits; always = immer; never =
noch nie, niemals; just = gerade

b *yet* steht am Satzende; die Anderen wie *ever*, *never*
stehen vor dem Partizip.

Test 85

Aufgabe 1

a Das *present perfect* wird für Handlungen oder Zustände verwandt, die in der Vergangenheit begonnen
haben und in die Gegenwart hineinreichen.

b Handlungen mit *just* sind kurz vor dem gegen-
wärtigen Zeitpunkt zu Ende gegangen. **Tipp:** Im
amerikanischen Englisch wird hier meistens das
simple past benutzt.

Aufgabe 2

1 They have bought a map.
2 They have planned their route.
3 They have cleaned their car.
4 They have prepared some sandwiches.
5 They have bought something to drink.
6 They have packed their bags.
7 They have put their bags in the car.
8 They have locked the door.
9 They have left a window open.

Test 86

Aufgabe 1

... we haven't stopped once ...
... we left this morning ...
... I haven't eaten anything either.
I had a sandwich this morning, but you didn't want
to eat ...
... what you said this morning. I had two ...

Aufgabe 2

was; couldn't; haven't caught; went; haven't already
thrown

Test 87

Aufgabe 1

a ... weather will be better.
There won't be any rain ...
There will be a lot of sunshine ...
But in the evening it will be cloudy.
There will be rain ...
Temperatures will be around 20 °C ...

b Das *will-future* drückt u. a. aus, dass etwas unabhängig
vom eigenen Wollen oder Hoffen in der Zukunft geschieht.

Aufgabe 2

a I think it will be pretty good today.
Probably it will be warmer later.
Probably it won't rain.
I hope there won't be a storm again.
I believe it will be rather windy, though.

b Diese Verben drücken eine Hoffnung oder Vermutung
aus.

Test 88

Aufgabe 1

1 b
2 c
3 a

Aufgabe 2

a Satz 1 ist sicher oder wahrscheinlich.
b

1 if
2 when
3 when
4 when

Test 89

Aufgabe 1

1 Are you going to work harder this term?
Yes, I am./No, I'm not.
2 Are you going to study more for your tests?
Yes, I am./No, I'm not.
3 Are you going to get better marks?
Yes, I am./No, I'm not.
4 Are you going to watch less TV?
Yes, I am./No, I'm not.
5 Are your friends going to help you?
Yes, they are./No, they aren't.

Aufgabe 2

Mögliche Antworten:
What are your parents going to buy?
Why are you going to call him?
When are your friends going to visit us?
Who is Debbie going to meet?
Where is Tom going to meet her?

Test 90

Aufgabe 1
1 richtig
2 richtig
3 richtig

Aufgabe 2
a will
b is going to
c is going to
d will
e will
f will
g will
h will
i is going to
j is going to
k will

Test 91

Aufgabe 1
a is
b has just come
c has got
d is unpacking
e has to
f was
g had to
h wasn't allowed to
i enjoyed
j could lie
k are going to go
l will be

Aufgabe 2
present oder past progressive
present perfect
simple present
simple past
will-future
going to-future

Test 92

Aufgabe 1
Who has come back?
Who has gone to school again?
Who doesn't feel well?
Who feels sad?
Who isn't happy?
What is over?
Who enjoyed the holidays?
Who didn't want to come back?
What is lying on the floor?
Who is going to go there again?

Aufgabe 2
a Bei Fragen nach dem Subjekt gebrauchst du *who* oder *what*.
b Das folgende Verb steht danach immer im Singular.
c Bei Fragen nach dem Subjekt darfst du im *simple present* oder im *simple past to do* nur in nicht verneinten Fragen gebrauchen.
d Bei Fragen nach anderen Satzteilen steht im *simple present* und im *simple past* immer die entsprechende Form von *to do*.

Test 93

Aufgabe 1
Who can she see again?
Who is waiting for her?
When will she see them?
What are they going to talk about?
Who can she see?
Who does she like?
What does she know?
What can they do together?

Aufgabe 2
1 Yes, I did.
2 Yes, I was.
3 No, I'm not.
4 Yes, I do.
5 No, I don't.
6 No, I haven't.
7 Yes, you can.
8 No, I haven't.
9 Yes, I am.
10 Yes, it will.

Test 94

Aufgabe 1
a Yesterday Debbie didn't feel well.
b But today Debbie feels better.
c Today she can see Tom again./She can see Tom again today.
d She is going to be at school at 8.30./At 8.30 she is going to be at school.
e So they will have enough time to see each other.

Aufgabe 2
When they see each other, they won't cry./
... they won't talk about school.
... they will laugh a lot.
... they will have fun together.
... they will be happy.

Test 95

Aufgabe 1
Are the children back?
Are two children ill?
Can't they come?
Did they catch a cold yesterday?
Are the teachers there, too?
Will lessons begin soon?
Is a teacher coming?
Does the classroom door open?
Do the pupils stand up?

Aufgabe 2
1 a vor diesen Formen
2 b nach dem ersten Teil des Prädikats
3 b falsch
4 a richtig

LÖSUNGEN

Test 96

Aufgabe 1

a Have you seen Tom?
   I can't find him.
   Yes, I have seen him.
   When I saw him, he was looking for Debbie.
   He was looking for a CD, too.

b Im Englischen stehen Objekte immer nach dem Verb oder der Verbgruppe.
   Im Deutschen trennt man Hilfsverb + Verb-Konstruktionen, sodass ein Objekt immer dazwischen liegt.

Aufgabe 2

I have just seen him.
He will go to Debbie's house again.
He will leave the house again.
He has forgotten something.
He must look for it.
He will find it.

Test 97

Aufgabe 1

On Tuesday he's going to study for a test.
On Wednesday he is going to play table tennis.
On Thursday, he is going to see Debbie.
On Friday, he is going to practice playing the guitar.
On Sunday he is going to watch a football match on TV.
On Sunday he is going to go to the cinema with Debbie.

Aufgabe 2

a Mögliche Lösungen:
   Tonight I'm going to learn French.
   On Monday I'm going to stay in bed.
   Next week I'm going to go to a pop concert.
   This school year I'm going to work more.
   This summer I'm going to go on holidays.
   In July I'm going to go to Spain.

b Sie stehen entweder am Satzanfang oder am Satzende.

Test 98

Aufgabe 1

a Near Tom's school there is a park/There is a park near Tom's school.
   He often goes there.
   It's not very far. He can walk there.
   There's a playground in the park.
   They can play in the park.

b am Satzende

c am Satzanfang

Aufgabe 2

a 1 In England pupils start school when they are five./Pupils start school in England when they are five.
   2 Most English pupils go to a comprehensive school when they are eleven./When they are eleven, most English pupils go to a comprehensive school.
   3 They can leave school when they are 16./When they are 16, they can leave school.
   4 In most schools lessons start at 8.30./Lessons start in most schools at 8.30.

b Die Reihenfolge ist immer Ort vor Zeit (place – time).

Test 99

Aufgabe 1

They are often loud.
They always run around.
They have never learned to sit still.
They never listen.
They usually forget their homework.
Have you ever met such people?
Sometimes they drive their teachers crazy./They sometimes drive their teachers crazy.

Aufgabe 2

a "I have to go", he said quietly.
b He slowly closed the door./He closed the door slowly.
c He carefully locked the door./He locked the door carefully.
d Then he quickly opened his bag./Then he opened his bag quickly.
e He quickly put the key in it./He put the key in it quickly.

Test 100

Aufgabe 1

a	whose	e	who
b	whose	f	who
c	which	g	who
d	which	h	which

Aufgabe 2

a	–	e	whose
b	–	f	–
c	which	g	–
d	–		

Test 101

Aufgabe 1

Debbie is the girl Tom is in love with.
Debbie is the girl he is interested in.
Debbie is the girl he dreams of.
Tom is the boy she is looking for.

Aufgabe 2
Do you know the film which is on TV tonight?
Do you know the actor who plays the main character in it?
Didn't Richard Gere play a part in the film you saw some days ago?
What was the title of the film he was in?
Didn't you see it with Debbie? You know the girl who is Tom's friend.

Test 102

Aufgabe 1
Debbie says that she is ill.
She explains that she has got the flu.
She adds that her mum called a doctor.
Tom answers that he is very sorry.
He says that he hopes that she doesn't feel very bad.
He thinks/is sure/believes that she will feel better soon.
He adds that he will tell Mr Mason that she is ill.

Aufgabe 2
Tom asks Debbie if she feels better today.
He wants to know if she can get up.
Then he asks her if the doctor came.
He wants to know if she has to stay in bed.
He also wants to know if he can come to see her.
Then he asks her if she has taken any medicine.

Test 103

Aufgabe 1
1 a) Fragen
2 b) to ask/c) to want to know
3 b) if
4 b) wie im Aussagesatz
5 b) nein
6 b) nein.

Aufgabe 2
Her mother wants to know if her friends can visit her.
She asks the doctor if she is very ill.
She wants to know if she has got the flu.
She wants to know if she feels very bad.
She asks if she has a temperature.
She asks him if she will get better soon.

Gute Gründe für Nachhilfe in Profi-Qualität

Erfolg in der Schule ist nicht zuletzt eine Frage der individuellen Förderung. Seit 40 Jahren setzt sich der Studienkreis dafür ein, Schülerinnen und Schülern Freude am Lernen zu vermitteln. Erfahrene und geprüfte Nachhilfelehrer unterstützen jeden einzelnen Schüler kompetent und einfühlsam auf seinem Weg zu besseren Noten.

Neben der Nachhilfe in allen Fächern bereiten wir auch gezielt auf Prüfungen vor und haben mit unserer Kinderlernwelt ein spezielles Förderangebot für Grundschulkinder. Der Studienkreis – einer der größten privaten Bildungsanbieter Europas – ist an rund 1.000 Standorten zu finden. Auch in Ihrer Nähe.

So sorgen wir für bessere Noten:

- Professionelle Lehrkräfte: fachlich und pädagogisch qualifiziert und gezielt ausgewählt
- Kostenlose Beratung durch erfahrene Ansprechpartner vor Beginn jeder Förderung
- Individuelle Lernpläne entsprechend den Bedürfnissen jedes einzelnen Kindes
- Top-Lernkonzept für bessere Noten: von Experten entwickelt und in rund 1.000 Standorten erfolgreich erprobt

Mehr Infos unter www.studienkreis.de oder Telefon 0800 111 12 12 (Mo.–Sa. 8–20 Uhr, gebührenfrei)

Jetzt testen!

Gute-Noten-Gutschein

für 4 kostenlose Probestunden* im Studienkreis

- Einzulösen im Studienkreis in Ihrer Nähe.
- Den nächstgelegenen Studienkreis finden Sie auf **www.studienkreis.de** und unter Telefon 0800 111 12 12 (Mo.–Sa. 8–20 Uhr, gebührenfrei)

*4 x 45 Minuten Unterricht als 2 Doppelstunden in einer kleinen, fachbezogenen Lerngruppe. Pro Person 1 Gutschein einlösbar. Nur für neue Schüler und nur in teilnehmenden Niederlassungen. Der Gutschein ist nicht mit anderen Angeboten kombinierbar.

Foto: © Studienkreis